GW00870726

CHILDREN'S
OF THE YI

1992
EDITION

Selected by Julia Eccleshare

ANDERSEN PRESS/CHILDREN'S BOOK FOUNDATION

© Children's Book Foundation 1992

Published by Andersen Press Limited in association with the
Children's Book Foundation in 1992
20 Vauxhall Bridge Road,
London SW1

ISBN 0 86264 395 3

The selected titles in this publication are available for hire as
a Book Trust touring exhibition. Contact the Head of Exhibitions,
Book Trust, Book House, 45 East Hill, London SW18 for details.

Cover illustration by Tony Ross

Typeset by 🅰 Tek Art Limited, Addiscombe, Croydon, Surrey
Printed in Great Britain by Courier International Limited, East Kilbride.

CHILDREN'S BOOKS OF THE YEAR 1992 EDITION

Key to symbols used

P = Paperback

1992 is Julia Eccleshare's eighth year as selector of *Children's Books of the Year*. She has been Children's Books Editor for the *Times Literary Supplement* (1974–78) and was Fiction Editor for Puffin Books (1978–79) and for Hamish Hamilton (1979–84).

She now works as a freelance reviewer, is married with four children and lives in London.

INTRODUCTION

Poised on the brink of joining our European neighbours in a union of some kind, it would be nice to think that the children's fiction for 1991 could be judged positively as a statement of this country's commitment to reading within a cultured and educated environment.

Alas, this year's fiction is published against a background of rhetoric and invective about how children should learn to read which, in turn, has a significant effect on *what* they read and on our whole concept of a literate society. The introduction of assessment tasks at seven, however they are dressed up, will inevitably push teachers towards 'teaching' which may in turn become 'bullying' children to learn to read with tricks and techniques which have little to do with the enjoyment of story or the understanding of the particular and special qualities of books. Given the international reputation Britain has for its children's publishing it seems ironic that it is barely recognised and certainly little valued in this country by those who could make it a powerful and creative tool where it would be most effective – in schools.

Fortunately, in some areas at least, authors, illustrators and publishers have kept faith with the true purpose of books for children. In picture books and poetry, most notably, there remains an understanding that children need to be taken places by what they read. Stories that feed the imagination still abound in picture books. Babette Cole's *Tarzanna* (10) builds on a presumption of some knowledge of the great mythical hero but then makes witty and imaginative leaps of its own. Allan and Janet Ahlberg weave stories around stories around stories in their brilliant *The Jolly Christmas Postman* (2), a book which extends the limits of what most people would recognise as possible for a picture book. Martin Waddell and Helen Oxenbury's *Farmer Duck* (48) captures the spirit of revolution and the rise of the oppressed in a simple but powerful picture book format. The choice in picture books is rich and varied and, thank goodness that it is, since this must be the best possible way of holding the dyke against the tidal wave of home learning programmes and reading schemes with which parents are daily tempted.

Poetry collections, too, remain steadfast to the imaginative ideal of literature. Maybe poetry has always had an extra licence to be whimsical. Certainly the abundance of good anthologies reflects a commitment to outstanding poetry without rejecting or forgetting that dead authors wrote well too. In *The Puffin Book of Twentieth-Century Children's Verse* (134) Brian

Patten gives readers the opportunity to step backwards in time through poetry by enjoying a wide range of poets from Richard Edwards and John Agard to Thomas Hardy. Michael Rosen adds cultural breadth in *A World of Poetry* (136) by including Afro-American and Egyptian poetry as well. The changing cultural basis of children's books is excellently reflected in Grace Nichols' collection of poems from Black, Asian and American Indian cultures, *Can I Buy A Slice of Sky?* (133), while the power of poetry as a medium for exploring contemporary issues is demonstrated convincingly in Anne Harvey's collection *Shades of Green* (130).

Poetry seems well able to retain the vital essence of imagination while also addressing contemporary issues. In fiction this seems to be considerably harder to achieve. A lack of confidence about what 'story' is *for* seems to pervade much of what is published for those readers who most desperately need to be first tempted, and then kept well nourished. In 'Getting Going' I have chosen stories which will help bridge the gap between feeling confident with a picture book text and managing a 'chapter' book alone. Children make these distinctions of appearance. Picture book readers may have just as comprehensive vocabularies but their perception of themselves changes when they feel able to read longer stories broken up into chapters. It is then that they see themselves as readers rather than learners and it is then that they need to become hooked by the habit. To do this, they require just the same stimulation visually, linguistically and imaginatively that they were getting from picture books.

I have tried to find stories, integrated with illustrations in a variety of ways, which will do this. Stories which are strong on character, drama and integrity. Stories which 'tell' well, driven by the desire of the writer to entertain the imagination of a child reader. The same ingredients lie behind my choices for 'Moving On' and 'Taking Off'. I have selected the books which make reading attractive and, above all, special. The literary standards and expectations which have lain behind the children's book tradition in this country have preserved reading. The danger lies in making reading as close to other media as possible in the mistaken belief that it will then be more attractive to children who, it is known, consume television visually and music aurally far more easily than they read. The best stories, well told, will make the fiction of the future and, I feel sure, provide the imaginative basis for future visual and aural delights.

Reinforcement for this argument comes from the upsurge in the past few years of collections of folk stories, stories which have the integrity of their heritage and, at their heart, the desire to entertain children with the telling of stories. That this combination is effective is proven by the fact that the stories are still well known today. This year two books, *Time for Telling* (57) retold by Mary Medlicott and *Bury My Bones But Keep My Words* (55) retold by Tony Fairman, have taken the folk story tradition one stage further by setting down 'told' stories in a written form, thus preserving some of the best stories for future generations.

From picture books through the intervening stages of fiction to poetry, this guide is designed for children of infant, primary and middle school age. The non-fiction has been selected for the same age group. The days of learning to read as part of the whole process of enjoying books may be numbered and, so too, may be the idea of learning laterally rather than in strict, subject-based measures. Even before that has happened, the non-fiction titles are largely single subject and have been chosen for their clarity and their enthusiasm. Even more than with fiction, a book cannot compete with other media. Glossy photographs are the nearest they can come to exciting television images but the strength of the book must lie in the way it captures the imagination of the reader as it informs. In this way children can learn creatively and with pleasure.

Reading is special and so are books. They are all too easily classified as luxuries, the prerogative of an educated elite. But reading is central to all understanding and good writing, though often dismissed as 'unavailable', is in reality no more difficult to read than bad. Carefully constructed 'literary' writing can often be more accessible than writing which purports to be easy because it closely resembles speech. The books in this year's selection are all good in as many ways as possible. They have all been chosen to support the cause of giving children, the readers of the future, the chance to revel in the printed word.

1
ADAMS, Ken
When I was Your Age
illustrated by Val Biro
Simon & Schuster Young Books
1991 £7.99 24pp.
0 7500 0450 9

Sammy's Grandpa makes some pretty outrageous claims. 'When I was your age I was so clever I could read my books with one eye closed and balancing on my head. At the same time I juggled sixteen cups and saucers with my toes and told the teacher the answers to all the sums she couldn't do. That's how clever I was.' Sammy is rightly sceptical until Grandpa's last claim which they both believe and enjoy equally. Val Biro's exuberant illustrations of an aged Grandpa showing off capture exactly the spirit of the affectionate interchange between old and young.

2
AHLBERG, Allan
AHLBERG, Janet
The Jolly Christmas Postman
Heinemann
1991 £9.99 28pp.
0 434 92532 2

To attempt to extend the joke so successfully introduced in *The Jolly Postman* was a bold move. To do it so brilliantly is a master stroke. 'Once upon a Christmas Eve/Just after it had snowed,/The Jolly Postman (him again!)/Came down the jolly road': thus, against a snowy and Christmassy background, the postman begins his round of important visits to Four Bears Cottage, Red Riding Hood's play house, the hospital for Humpty Dumpty and some more. His letters are gifts in themselves, each made up of a series of seemingly endless witty plays on the traditional fairy story ideas.

3
ALLEN, Pamela
Black Dog
Hamish Hamilton
1991 £8.50 32pp.
0 241 13138 3

The intensity of the emotion captured in the illustrations makes *Black Dog* a book with a powerful impact. Christina and Black Dog are the best of friends but when Christina catches a fleeting glimpse of a bright blue bird outside her window she can think of nothing else. Black Dog lies hungry and neglected until he takes the most enormous risk, just to show Christina that he, too, is important and special.

4
ANHOLT, Catherine
ANHOLT, Laurence
What I Like
Walker
1991 £7.99 24pp.
0 7445 1946 2

Children's likes and dislikes, as seen by six children but with a universality which makes them appealing to all. 'I love . . . whales and snails, dogs and frogs . . .' The twins sometimes don't like 'being a pair, people who stare, having to share'. The scant, rhyming text is elegantly fleshed out by delicate illustrations full of tiny details.

5
APPIAH, Sonia
Amoko and the Party
illustrated by Carol Easmon
Andre Deutsch
1991 £5.99 32pp.
0 233 98530 1

Set in Ghana, *Amoko and the Party* is a tender story of how a family celebrates a birthday. The birthday is Mansah's and the biggest present of all will be her father's homecoming after a long time away. Seen from Amoko's perspective it tells of the build up – mother's new dress to be collected from the dressmaker, everyone getting washed and changed, getting a present ready, and the party itself – the food, drink, dancing and happiness. With its own, strong Ghanaian identity *Amoko and the Party* shows family warmth and interaction anywhere.

6
BROWNE, Anthony
Willy and Hugh
Julia MacRae
1991 £6.99 24pp.
0 85681 030 5

Willy, eponymous hero of *Willy the Wimp* and *Willy the Champ*, is back, finding out about friends and friendship. The simplicity of the text and of Anthony Browne's daringly empty illustrations should not deceive readers into thinking that this is a book for young readers only. Browne's statements about relationships and the different ways that people need each other will speak clearly to all age groups.

7
BURNINGHAM, John
Aldo
Cape
1991 £7.99 32pp.
0 224 03116 3

Full of sorrow, *Aldo* is also a book which will reassure all those who need or have a secret friend. Lonely and timid, a little girl has the consolation of her special friend Aldo who is always there whenever she needs him. In stunning, magical double-page spreads, John Burningham shows the secret world Aldo and the girl inhabit where they can find peace and obvious total happiness.

8
CARLE, Eric
The Secret Birthday
Message
Hamish Hamilton
1991 £7.99 24pp.
0 241 12533 2

Eric Carle's clever use of cut pages to give a range of shapes to explore and unfold until the final code is cracked, makes *The Secret Birthday Message* a picture book of imagination and depth. Carle's richly textured illustrations bring the shapes to life for Tim, in his search for his birthday surprise, and for the readers who search with him.

9
CHICHESTER CLARK,
Emma
Tea with Aunt Augusta
Methuen
1991 £6.99
0 416 17002 1

A small slice of bushbaby family life is wittily and charmingly captured in both the text and illustrations of this visually striking picture book. Eagerly, the bushbabies set out for tea with their Aunt Augusta. Greedily, Jemima eats as much as she can. So much that, what with feeling sick and the extra weight she is carrying, she gets left miles behind the others on the way home. Luckily (and beautifully) the bats come to her rescue and guide her safely home. The dark bats with their glowing white eyes against the green jungle background make the most striking images.

10
COLE, Babette
Tarzanna
Hamish Hamilton
1991 £7.99 32pp
0 241 13133 2

Babette Cole is at her imaginative best in *Tarzanna*, the story of the jungle girl who lets loose the animals in the zoo with dramatic and unexpected results. The storyline is amusing, as much for what it leaves out as for what it includes, and the visual jokes make it a book which can be readily enjoyed through the pictures alone.

11
COWCHER, Helen
Tigress
Andre Deutsch
1991 £7.99 36pp.
0 233 98677 4

Visually powerful with its bold, brightly coloured Tigress and its coolly simple portrayal of the barely sustainable life of the peasant and his flock, *Tigress* also contains a powerful message. Within the confines of a brief text Helen Cowcher poses clearly the problems of protecting natural predators in a country where the land is desperately needed by the growing population of peasants who are struggling for their own survival.

12
FRENCH, Fiona
Anancy and Mr Dry Bone
Frances Lincoln
1991 £7.95 32pp.
0 7112 0672 4

Fiona French's stark but stylish illustrations give enormous vigour to this richly-set retelling of an Anancy story. Rich Mr Dry Bone and poor Anancy both love the beautiful Miss Louise. But it is not money that will buy her love. Whoever makes her laugh will be the one to win her. Helped by Tiger, Monkey, Dog, Crocodile and Parrot, Anancy wears a costume of such originality and absurdity that Miss Louise bursts out laughing at the sight of him.

13
FRONT, Sheila
Jacob and the Noisy
Children
illustrated by Charles Front
Andre Deutsch
1991 £6.99 32pp.
0 233 98627 8

Noisy children may make your house seem unbearable but noisy children and pets are even worse. So Jacob the tailor finds when he follows the Rabbi's advice and gets pets for his children in an attempt to win some peace for himself. Adult readers will readily identify with Jacob while children will be amused by the antics of his children in this culturally rich moral tale of counting your blessings.

14
GABAN, Jesus
BARKOW, Henriette
(reteller)
Abdul and the Lion
Mantra
1991 £7.95 32pp.
1 85269 106 9

Abdul, the young shepherd, plays his flute in the lonely watches of the night and is visited by the King of the Mountains – the last black-maned lion. Abdul is not afraid and he and the lion travel through the Atlas Mountains living alongside the animals who live there. But Abdul's hunger causes him to lead the lion into danger. Man destroys the fine balance that the animals preserve among themselves. Jesus Gaban's stunning illustrations bring the secrets of the mountains to life while also conveying the need to preserve the balance of nature.

15
GIFFARD, Hannah
Red Fox
Frances Lincoln
1991 £6.95 24pp.
0 7112 0641 4

The bold outlines and bright colours of the stylized woodblock illustrations make *Red Fox* an original visual drama as well as a pleasingly familiar story of a fox's night of scavenging.

16
GRAHAM, Bob
Greetings from Sandy
Beach
Blackie
1991 £6.95 32pp.
0 216 93168 1

A family holiday, warts and all, is the theme of *Greetings from Sandy Beach*. Bob Graham's skill lies in his effective use of an understated text which is given expression in his bubbling and witty illustrations. He captures how a child looks at such things, poking gentle fun at parents.

17
GRANT, Gwen
Little Blue Car
illustrated by Susan Hellard
Orchard
1991 £7.99 32pp.
0 85213 303 1

Quaintly old-fashioned in feel, *The Little Blue Car* is also a book of particular charm and warmth. The adventurous little blue car longs to see the wide world outside the factory gates. Boldly he sets off but quickly discovers that life is more frightening than he had suspected. Older and wiser vehicles help him find his way back to the safety of the factory. A simple exploration of some important, childish feelings. Susan Hellard's illustrations give clearly defined character to the tractor, bus, lorry and especially to the little blue car itself.

18
HARVEY, Amanda
Stormy Weather
Macmillan
1991 £6.99 32pp.
0 333 54944 9

Amanda Harvey's gentle and atmospheric illustrations tell this original story of how a young girl and an old woman set out to collect the last blackberries of the year. Together, they watch Winter as he comes sweeping along with his rake, singing his chilly song. Defying him, they collect their blackberries which they savour, knowing that they are the last of the year. A book for older readers to linger over, and enjoy the spare text which matches the mood of the illustrations perfectly.

19
HAYES, Sarah
This is the Bear and the
Scary Night
illustrated by Helen Craig
Walker
1991 £6.99 32pp.
0 7445 1943 8

Poor Bear gets forgotten in the park and has some scary adventures before he is happily rescued from the pond and reunited with his forgetful but loving owner. Sarah Hayes' rhyming text is as charming as in the two previous 'Bear' titles and Helen Craig captures exactly the changing moods and overall tenderness and wit.

20
HEIDE, Florence Parry
GILLILAND, Judith
Heide
The Day of Ahmed's
Secret
illustrated by Ted Lewin
Gollancz
1991 £7.99 24pp.
0 575 05079 9

The sights, sounds and smells of the daily life of Cairo are richly conveyed in Ted Lewin's detailed and atmospheric illustrations and in the text which captures, too, Ahmed's pent-up excitement about the secret he is dying to share. This picture book story also offers a window into the childhood of a boy from another country and culture.

21
HISSEY, Jane
Jolly Snow
Hutchinson
1991 £7.99 32pp.
0 09 176414 9

Jolly Tall, Little Bear, Duck, Rabbit, Zebra and the rest are waiting and waiting for the snow to fall. But it is such a long time coming that Little Bear decides to invent his own snow. Snow bubbles, paper snowflakes, a sleigh run made from a sheet – the animals find lots of ways to enjoy their own 'snow', so much so that when the real stuff comes they are not sure they want to go out after all. Set in a cosy but not twee toy world, Jane Hissey has created a rich cast of characters, drawn in exquisite detail.

22
HOFFMAN, Mary
Amazing Grace
illustrated by Caroline Binch
Frances Lincoln
1991 £7.95 32pp.
0 7122 0670 8

Caroline Binch's beautiful and vigorous illustrations powerfully project the image of Grace who, with the support of her mother and her grandmother, discovers that you can do anything that you want to. In this case it is getting the part of Peter Pan in the school play. Mary Hoffman has written a warm story that contains important messages about self-motivation and challenging stereotypes.

23
IKEDA, Daisaku
McCAUGHREAN,
Geraldine (translator)
The Princess and the
Moon
illustrated by
Brian Wildsmith
Oxford
1991 £6.95 24pp.
0 19 271680 8

Transported to the moon by the beautiful moon rabbit, Sophie finds herself in a magical world where all the children wear flowing capes and crowns of gold. No one is cross or quarrelling. All are smiling, happy, singing and dancing. One in particular – a princess – captures Sophie's attention. Her face is so familiar. It is the one Sophie sees herself, every time she looks in the mirror. Can it really be her? Together, text and illustrations weave a magical spell as this story of inner and outer selves is unravelled.

24
INKPEN, Mick
Kipper
Hodder & Stoughton
1991 £5.99 24pp.
0 340 54053 2

Mick Inkpen's lovable puppy, Kipper, is dissatisfied with his own basket. Even when he has thrown out his old ball and bone, his soft rabbit and his smelly old blanket he cannot get comfortable. Where can he find a comfier place to sleep? Observing the animals around him, Kipper experiments with a bird's nest, a frog's lily pad, a rabbit's hole and much more besides. Nothing is quite right for a puppy. Kipper returns to his own basket and snuggles down with all his favourite things around him. Well-shaped and nicely told, *Kipper* is an attractive variation on a familiar theme.

25
ISADORA, Rachel
At the Crossroads
Julia MacRae
1991 £7.99 32pp.
1 85681 122 0

All night the children wait for their fathers to come home from working in the mines. They have been away for ten months and the children's excitement is barely containable. There are so many things that fathers are needed for. Rachel Isadora's text is minimal but through it and her richly coloured illustrations of the day and night of waiting she conveys a strong sense of people and place.

26
JAMES, Simon
Jake and the Babysitter
Macmillan
1991 £6.99 32pp.
0 333 53787 4

Jake's babysitter does some pretty unusual things – for a regular babysitter. Raiding the fridge, jumping on the beds and watching a really scary horror film on TV are all things that are usually frowned on by babysitters. But who exactly *is* Jake's unusual minder anyway? Simon James mixes fear with enough humour to be reassuring.

27
JONAS, Ann
Aardvarks, Disembark!
Julia MacRae
1991 £7.99
1 85681 000 3

Ann Jonas brings fresh light to the story of Noah and his ark while also supplying a wealth of information about unfamiliar animals from all over the world. After forty days and nights the water has receded sufficiently for Noah, his family and all the animals to step out onto dry land. 'Aardvarks, disembark!' calls Noah. But even after he has got to 'zebra', Noah finds his ark full of animals whose names he does not even know. Out pour the most fantastic display of exotic, and often now extinct, animals. Each is exquisitely drawn and the device of them getting larger and larger on the page success-fully works in making them look as if they are really coming out of the ark.

28
KEMP, Gene
Matty's Midnight Monster
illustrated by Diann Timms
Faber
1991 £7.99 32pp.
0 571 14336 9

Matty is frightened by the thought of the story with a monster in it but she is tempted, too. One night she borrows the book from Granny and lets the monster out. How Matty tames the monster, sending him shrinking back into the pages where he belongs, makes a vivid story which well reflects the power of the printed word and the influence that stories should have.

29
KENNAWAY, Adrienne
Bushbaby
Hamish Hamilton
1991 £7.99 24pp.
0 241 13060 3

Set in a brilliant green forest populated by colobus monkeys, a shy genet, praying mantis and thousands of ants, *Bushbaby* is the story of how the greedy but lovable Bushbaby ignores danger in his craving for the ripest and juiciest figs. While Bushbaby feasts himself Monitor waits below lashing his tail and shooting out his long, forked tongue. Bushbaby must take one giant leap right out of the tree and home to the safety of his mother. Adrienne Kennaway's illustrations are vibrant and capture the secret world of the forest.

30
LESTER, Alison
Imagine
Viking
1991 £7.99 24pp.
0 670 83692 3

'Imagine if we were deep in the jungle . . . if we were like fish in the ocean . . . crossing the icecap . . . out in the country . . . surrounded by monsters . . .' Each double-page spread creates a complete new world, stuffed full of animals from different countries, climates and times. Rich in visual detail, each picture is surrounded by a border of identifying words.

31
LIONNI, Leo
Matthew's Dream
Andersen
1991 £7.99 32pp.
0 86264 322 8

The effect of art on Matthew, a young mouse of humble origins, lies at the centre of this beautiful and profound story. Leo Lionni's brilliant use of collage demonstrates clearly how looking closely at painting inspires changes in how you look at your own life and interpret dreams. Sparely told, *Matthew's Dream* is, nonetheless, a book with enormous impact.

32
LIPNIACKA, Ewa
To Bed . . . or Else!
illustrated by Basia Bogdanowicz
Magi
1991 £6.99 32pp.
1 85430 195 0

Ewa Lipniacka humorously captures the familiar confrontation between Mum and children at bedtime. Hannah and Asha love to spend nights with each other but, when they can't settle to sleep, Mum starts counting . . . What *will* Mum do if they are not asleep by the time she has reached three? Hannah and Asha's imagination gives them more than enough to worry about.

33
LOCKHART SMITH,
Cara
Twenty-six Rabbits Go
Crackers
Orchard
1991 £7.99 32pp.
1 85213 261 2

With twenty-six rabbits (including the baby) to look after it is surprising that Mrs Rabbit looks as calm as she does, especially since it is Christmas Eve. Luckily Mrs Rabbit has an easy-going temperament so that, with just a few mishaps on the way, the whole family hurtle excitedly towards Christmas. The sheer good-naturedness of the rabbit family combined with their numbers makes this book full of all kinds of happy visual treats.

34
MACAULAY, David
Why the Chicken
Crossed the Road
Collins
1991 £7.99 32pp.
0 00 193490 2

Bold illustrations tell this carefully constructed, elaborate and witty explanation of the title. David Macaulay includes enough detail to be visually amusing while never labouring the serious points about cause and effect that he is making on the way.

35
McKEE, David
Elmer Again
Andersen
1991 £6.99 24pp.
0 86264 326 0

Following the success of *Elmer*, the story of the multi-coloured elephant who loves playing tricks on his fellow elephants, David McKee has introduced a new story on the same theme. On Elmer's Day all the elephants are painted Elmer colours, but who then is the real Elmer? Elmer's tricks are entertaining for elephants and readers alike.

36
MANSFIELD, Michael
Whale Boy
illustrated by Maggie
Raynor
Mantra
1991 £7.95 32pp.
1 85269 107 7

Packed full of important information about whales and the urgent need to save them, *Whale Boy* is also a vivid picture book with an imaginative text. Wadiike's speculation about saving whales leads him into a powerful dream world through which he experiences at first hand how whales live and their terrifying and tragic plight. Can Wadiike, in his waking life, save those whales from the threat of extinction? Maggie Raynor's underwater dream sequences bring the whales' world into fresh focus.

37
MOLLEL, Tololwa M.
The Orphan Boy
illustrated by Paul Morin
Oxford
1991 £6.95 32pp.
0 19 540783 0

The lyrical writing and richly textured illustrations which match it perfectly make *The Orphan Boy* a book to savour. Retelling a Maasai story which explains why the planet Venus is called Kileken, the orphan boy, it is a rare story of the love of an old man for the young son he never had. The emphasis is on the importance of trust and the fatality of breaking it. Paul Morin's illustrations give a detailed and unsentimental insight into the precarious but unruffled life of the Maasai.

38
PRATER, John
Lots To Do
Dent
1991 £6.95 32pp.
0 460 88073   X

Ordinary and boring household jobs are turned into something enjoyable in this fantasy of becoming a circus juggler with the washing-up, a mountaineer with moving junk up the stairs, a racing driver with the supermarket trolley and a lion tamer when cleaning out the rabbit. Each wordless fantasy is full of drama and surprise which prevents the somewhat repetitive device from becoming tedious.

39
RAY, Jane
The Story of Christmas
Orchard
1991 £8.99 28pp.
1 85213 208 9

Jane Ray's stunning illustrations are a clever and rewarding combination of immediate appeal as traditional illuminations and long-term delight as pictures to dwell on, providing a never-ending supply of detail. With a text, taken slightly bittily from the Bible, Jane Ray tells the story of the birth of Christ with the full panoply of angels, shepherds and, shown crossing a glorious greeny sea, the three kings. With its strong, if somewhat sanitised, Middle Eastern setting Jane Ray offers an attractive and genuine vision of Christmas.

40
ROSS, Tony
Don't Do That!
Andersen
1991 £6.99 24pp.
0 86264 344 9

Tony Ross has a gift for making a grotesque subject into a hilarious picture book. This time it is the universally abhorred habit of nose picking. Nellie's nose is a beautiful one. It wins her first prize in the nose competition and a part in the school play. But Nellie can't resist picking it. All extreme measures to get her finger unstuck fail dismally until Henry adopts a simple, painless but effective remedy. Nose picking will never be the same for children who have read *Don't Do That!*

41
SCHERMBRUCKER,
Reviva
Charlie's House
illustrated by Niki Daly
Walker
1991 £7.99 24pp.
0 7445 1519   X

Both as a picture of the absolute poverty of life in an African township and as an insight into a child's world of dreams, *Charlie's House* is tender and telling. Charlie's home is a leaky tin shelter but his house is a work of art. Created out of mud, old plastic bags and cardboard scraps it has a lounge, a kitchen, a bathroom and a bedroom that is just for Charlie. Charlie's imagination and creativity give him freedom and power.

42
SMEE, Nicola
Finish the Story, Dad
Walker
1991 £6.99 28pp.
0 7445 1926 8

Humorously moral, *Finish the Story, Dad* tells of the amazing adventures that Ruby gets sucked into all because her dad refuses to finish the story. With the story unfinished, Ruby cannot get to sleep, but Dad isn't the only person who refuses to read. Ruby asks a lion, who gives her a ride instead, a snake who gives her a swing, a gorilla, a crocodile, a giraffe and a bird but no one will finish the story. Nicola Smee tells a neat story, making her point without preaching.

43
SNAPE, Juliet
SNAPE, Charles
Frog Odyssey
Julia MacRae
1991 £7.99 24pp.
1 85681 200 6

Told partly through wonderful, frog-view illustrations of the world and partly through very realistic illustrations of the frogs themselves, *Frog Odyssey* is a neatly told story of survival. The frogs' pond is threatened by the builders. In order to save their tadpoles and build for the future, they must find a new home. A life threatening trek follows until, at last, they find the perfect refuge.

44
STEIG, William
Spinky Sulks
Gollancz
1991 £7.95 32pp.
0 575 05080 2

William Steig brilliantly conveys what it feels like to be in a sulk, what effect it has on the rest of the family and how hard it is to come out of it. Part of his skill lies in the fact that he doesn't judge either Spinky for sulking or the rest of his family for causing him to sulk. Throughout the story there is a wry humour, cleverly linguistically expressed in the text and perfectly reinforced in the illustrations.

45
STRAUSS, Gwen
The Night Shimmy
illustrated by Anthony
Browne
Julia MacRae
1991 £7.99 24pp.
1 85681 011 9

The power of a secret friend is expressively described in Anthony Browne's illustrations of Eric and the Night Shimmy who protects him from all the things he doesn't like, especially talking. When Eric meets Marcia he finds he no longer needs the Night Shimmy but he is not quite ready to lose him. The transition is delicate. Contrasting bold colour with muted and subdued effects makes the telling of this story a visual experience with a powerful effect and a wealth of images to work through.

46
VELTHUIJS, Max
Crocodile's Masterpiece
Andersen
1991 £6.99 24pp.
0 86264 351 1

When Elephant can't choose which of Crocodile's pictures he wants, Crocodile sells him a completely white canvas. Elephant happily sees whatever he pleases. His life is enriched and he is happy – until he discovers that he can see just the same pictures whether the white canvas is in front of him or not . . . Crocodile's hoax is more clever than cruel while Elephant is an endearing innocent.

47
VYNER, Sue
VYNER, Tim
The Stolen Egg
Gollancz
1991 £7.99 32pp.
0 575 05155 8

Visually, *The Stolen Egg* is a delight as beautiful watercolours tell the story of how an egg is stolen, again and again, before it is luckily returned to its rightful owner. The albatross is the first thief, impelled to steal because someone has taken *her* egg. But there are other predators around – snakes, crocodiles, ostriches, tortoises – each of whom takes the egg for a while. The text of the story does little more than carry the powerful conservation message of the book reinforced by some factual information which sits a little uncomfortably at the end.

48
WADDELL, Martin
Farmer Duck
illustrated by Helen Oxenbury
Walker
1991 £8.99 32pp.
0 7445 1928 4

The exceptional quality of both text and illustrations, the integration of the two and the outstanding production of both make *Farmer Duck* a book to linger over. Martin Waddell's text is simple and spare but it carries a powerful message. Unfortunate duck works for a lazy, good-for-nothing farmer who lies in bed eating chocolates all day. Duck fetches the cow from the field, brings the sheep in from the hill, puts the hens in their house and does all the odd jobs around the farm. 'The poor duck was sleepy and weepy and tired.' Nothing could look more forlorn than Helen Oxenbury's weary and tearful duck as it lies slumped on a pile of hay being petted by the hens. Enough is enough. The farm animals take matters into their own hands, chase out the farmer and run the farm themselves as a happy co-operative. Helen Oxenbury brings exactly the right humour and pathos to this original interpretation of 'It's not fair'.

49
WADDELL, Martin
Let's Go Home, Little Bear
illustrated by Barbara Firth
Walker
1991 £8.99 32pp.
0 7445 1912 8

A trip home through the snowy woods is fun for Little Bear until he begins to be alarmed by all the noises around him. Luckily, Big Bear is there to reassure him that the sinister sounding Dripper is nothing more than the ice dripping in the stream, the frightening Plopper is only the snow dripping from the branch while the WOO WOO WOO and the CREAK CREAK CREAK are just the wind and the trees. As in its predecessor, *Can't You Sleep, Little Bear?*, the text and illustrations capture the cosy relationship between the two bears, this time against a beautiful snowy background.

50
WELLS, Rosemary
Max's Dragon Shirt
Collins
1991 £6.99 24pp.
0 00 193543 7

How Max outmanoeuvres his sister Ruby on a shopping trip will strike many familiar chords with anyone who has ever taken a child shopping. Max loves his old blue dungarees but 'They are disgusting' says Ruby. Off they go on a shopping trip with just enough money to buy the dungarees and not the dragon shirt which is what Max *really* wants. But, Ruby is tempted herself and, by losing Max, she also loses her control over what he is going to buy. Rosemary Wells captures exactly the interaction between Max and Ruby against an accurately observed shopping background.

51
WILLIS, Jeanne
Dr Xargle's Book of Earth
Mobiles
illustrated by Tony Ross
Andersen
1991 £6.99 32pp.
0 86264 339 2

In Dr Xargle's latest lesson, he turns his attention to the extraordinary vagaries of how humans travel. Horse riding, cycling ('The bicycle is popular. The earthling must hang on to the prongs and move his knees up and down. He must put a metal clip around his leg to prevent the bicycle eating the trouser.'), driving, sailing, flying and travelling by train are all given his best attention. As in the three previous titles Jeanne Willis's text is brilliantly funny. Few humans will be able to resist laughing.

52
WILSDORF, Anne
Lewis, Naomi
(translator)
Philomena
Bodley Head
1991 £8.99 32pp.
0 370 31598 7

How the bold Philomena defeats the witch is wittly told in subtle comic style in the illustrations and in the light and exuberant text. Full of fairy tale images with witches, monsters and a young heroine, this is also a book full of surprises and upsets, without recource to obvious role reversal.

53
CHARLES, Faustin
The Kiskadee Queen
illustrated by Lis Toft
Blackie
1991 £7.95 32pp.
0 216 93163 0

Animal rhymes, lullabies, action rhymes – Charles Faustin has collected together nursery verse from the Caribbean, India, Africa and Afro-American traditions. Set in their own culture with local topography, animals and work patterns, many also have distinct similarities with the traditional rhymes of this country. Lis Toft's illustrations are full of warmth and tenderness.

54
CROSSLEY-HOLLAND, Kevin (reteller)
Tales From Europe
BBC Books
1991 £9.99 104pp.
0 563 34795 3

Legends and fairy stories are here set alongside one another, allowing a glimpse into different storytelling traditions. Kevin Crossley-Holland has imposed a strong contemporary voice onto each, giving the stories an up-to-date flavour while retaining something of their origins. How Persephone comes to live three months of every year in the underworld, the story of the Ugly Duckling, the legend of King Arthur and the sword in the stone, how the Pied Piper of Hamelin led all the children from the town – these are the best known of the tales. From Switzerland comes 'The Army of Bears' explaining something of the history of Berne, and from Czechoslovakia another tale of a different kind of underworld, 'Godfather Death'. The stories probably work best individually rather than being taken as a whole. The illustrations are both ugly and distracting.

55
FAIRMAN, Tony (reteller)
Bury My Bones But Keep My Words
illustrated by Meshack Asare
Collins
1991 £9.99 192pp.
0 00 184988 3

Taken from all over Africa, this is a culturally rich collection of stories which, ideally, should be adapted by each 'reader' into their own words or voice, so keeping them within the storytelling tradition from which they come. But, whether read aloud or retold, they are all marvellous and original stories some with obvious European counterparts, such as the Omutugwa, a Luhya tale from Kenya, but most are quite new though with recognisable moral messages.

56
FOREMAN, Michael
Michael Foreman's
Mother Goose
Walker
1991 £12.99 152pp.
0 7445 0775 8

Michael Foreman's *Mother Goose* is a classic collection of many of the best traditional rhymes. Carefully grouped across double-page spreads the book begins and ends with lullabies while in between it is packed full of counting rhymes, singing rhymes, simple ballads and story poems. The varied moods of the poems are diversely illustrated in Michael Foreman's tender but never sentimental illustrations.

57
MEDLICOTT, Mary
(selector)
Time for Telling
illustrated by Sue Williams
Kingfisher
1991 £8.95 92pp.
0 86272 804 5

Designed to spur parents to read aloud and from there to develop their own skills as storytellers, this is a rich collection of stories selected from a range of backgrounds. 'How the Turtle Lost Her Sandals' is an Amerindian creation legend from Guyana, beautifully retold by Grace Nichols. Duncan Williamson's version of 'The Hedgehog's Race', a Scottish travellers' tale, tells how the hedgehog outwitted the hare in a race that was as much about cunning as running. Each of the stories has a particular resonance which makes them particularly effective when read aloud.

58
ROSEN, Michael
How the Animals Got
Their Colours
illustrated by John
Clementson
Studio Editions
1991 £7.95 48pp.
1 85170 730 1

Nine imaginative stories from around the world tell how different animals got their colours. The story of the Leopard comes from Liberia, the Crane from Uganda, the Peacock from India and the Tiger from China. Michael Rosen uses different styles for different stories (some are closer to poems than stories) which gives each story distinction and an identity of its own.

59
WATERS, Fiona
(compiler)
Stories for Bedtime
illustrated by Penny Dann
Orchard
1991 £8.99 80pp.
1 85213 243 4

The twelve stories in this collection reflect the high quality of storytelling available to even the youngest children. The humour of 'Cheese, Peas and Chocolate Pudding', the fantasy of 'The Beast with a Thousand Teeth', the tenderness of 'Big Sister and Little Sister' – each story has a clear identity which is also captured in Penny Dann's attractive illustrations. Not to be restricted to bedtime, this is a collection which will be enormously satisfying at any time of the day.

60
WINDHAM, Sophie
(illustrator)
The Orchard Book of
Nursery Stories
Orchard
1991 £9.99 96pp.
1 85213 189 6

Beautiful, finely drawn illustrations give charm to this attractively produced collection of fifteen familiar nursery stories. 'The Gingerbread Boy', 'Goldilocks and the Three Bears', 'The Three Billy Goats Gruff' – each of these stories and the others in the collection is told in a straightforward and uncluttered version which retains the traditional feel within an easy to understand vocabulary.

61
AIKEN, Joan
The Shoemaker's Boy
illustrated by Alan Marks
Simon & Schuster Young Books
1991 £2.99 46pp.
0 7500 0798 2 **P**

In the best fairy tale tradition, Jem must make an instinctive choice between good and evil. Being a good boy he makes the right choice, thus saving his dying mother and impoverished father. Joan Aiken's tale of this poor shoemaker's son and his mysterious and frightening night visitors is a vivid drama, lyrically told.

62
BAUDET, Stephanie
The Incredible Shrinking Hippo
illustrated by Debi Gliori
Hamish Hamilton
1991 £4.99 32pp.
0 241 12963 X

Lots of verbal play in this funny story about Simon who finds a hippopotamus in the garden. A hippopotamus is too big to have as a pet, but this one is magic. It shrinks whenever anyone says a word meaning small but grows back to its full size if anyone says hippopotamus. Keeping that under control shouldn't be difficult, thinks Simon, but it is surprising how much trouble he gets into.

63
BLACKMAN, Marjorie
Girl Wonder and the Terrific Twins
illustrated by Lis Toft
Gollancz
1991 £6.99 69pp.
0 575 05048 9

Maxine, Anthony and Edward have a knack of getting into trouble. Their good ideas often seem to have disastrous results. There is their plan to keep everyone cool at the swimming pool which ends up with several people getting unexpectedly wet. Rescuing Syrup the cat ends up with their own embarrassing rescue by the fire brigade. Saving energy seems to produce all the wrong results, while Maxine's effort at quick growth just give her a stomach ache. Marjorie Blackman has written some sparkling stories about three likeable, if accident prone, children.

64
FINE, Anne
Design a Pram
illustrated by Philippe
Dupasquier
Heinemann
1991 £2.99 48pp.
0 434 97672 5

Set to design a pram, the class divides into two groups led by the two rival bossies, Oliver and Hetty. After some swapping of sides, the two groups come up with two wonderfully contrasting designs – one safe and swaddling, the other more like a carriage of war. How can Mr Oakley possibly choose between the two? Anne Fine's classroom is full of convincing and engaging characters through whom she makes shrewd comments on stereotyping.

65
GIRLING, Brough
Clever Trevor
illustrated by Tony Blundell
A. & C. Black
1991 £4.95 64pp.
0 7136 3302 6

The skilful shared storytelling between text and pictures makes *Clever Trevor* a book that can be read and enjoyed on a number of different levels. Looking after a parrot should not be too difficult, but Trevor is not any old dumb bird. There is Trouble with the School Secretary, Trouble at Registration, Trouble at Assembly and Big Trouble with the Head Teacher, all because Trevor cannot keep his big beak shut. But being such a rude parrot is also what leads Trevor to unexpected glory. Samantha's dreadful experiences with her uncle's pet make hilarious reading.

66
HARRIS, Carmen
The Big Red Trouble
illustrated by Patricia
Ludlow

Richard wants the Scarleton XR2 that is in the junk shop window so much that he steals to pay for it. Surely Dad won't miss £5 from his wallet? And Richard does mean to pay it back. But how can he explain having the car in the meantime

Heinemann
1991 £2.99 48pp.
0 434 97679 2

and how can he enjoy it? Richard has to find a way of getting rid of the car and getting Dad's £5 back as quickly as possible in this carefully thought out moral dilemma.

67
KAYE, Geraldine
Snow Girl
illustrated by Joanna Carey
Heinemann
1991 £2.99 48pp.
0 434 97659 8

Why do people always build snowmen? After an exceptionally heavy snowfall the children at Hill Street School are all busy building for a competition. Tashi dreams of winning the beautiful toboggan that will be the first prize but her snowman is a snowgirl and for some reason that just won't do. Luckily the Lord Mayor (who is a lady) takes a hand and Tashi gets her toboggan after all. Geraldine Kaye has written a dramatic story that is full of understanding.

68
JARMAN, Julia
Nancy Pocket and the Kidnappers
illustrated by Jean Baylis
Heinemann
1991 £2.99 48pp.
0 434 97674 1

The arrival of a new baby in the family, especially when it is three at once, can be traumatic for a child of any age and Julia Jarman's adventure story makes an excellent framework for exploring those feelings. Nancy finds little to like about her three new noisy, sticky and smelly brothers and sister. The house now seems to be full of their things and even her room is no longer safe as soon as they start crawling. But, when the triplets are kidnapped, Nancy discovers just how much they mean to her and it is her brave and daring trick that leads to their rescue.

69
JUNGMAN, Ann
Leila's Magical Monster Party
illustrated by Doffy Weir
Viking
1991 £4.50 80pp.
0 670 83380 0

Leila gives a most unusual birthday party. Her guests do not have good reputations and some of them are known to be very troublesome indeed. A Wolf, a Giant, Ali Baba plus his forty thieves, two exceptionally Ugly Sisters, Leila invites them all with some catastrophic results. Ann Jungman gives substance to some favourite characters and wittily explores the relationship between fiction and reality.

**70
MARSHALL, James**
Fox at Work
Bodley Head
1991 £5.50 48pp.
0 370 31482 4

When Fox wrecks his bike he thinks his mother will just buy him a new one. But Mum has other ideas. Fox must get a job and earn some money to buy himself a new bike. Fox's attempts at getting – and keeping – jobs are wittily described in both text and illustrations. James Marshall offers exactly what is needed for readers who want a sophisticated storyline told in a simple vocabulary.

**71
MAYNE, William**
Rings On Her Fingers
illustrated by Thelma Lambert
Hamish Hamilton
1991 £3.99 42pp.
0 241 13071 9

In the midst of all the preparations for Christmas, Mum's jewellery goes missing. Josie obviously knows something about it. Did she swallow it? Did she bury it? Did she hide it away in a secret place and forget all about it? Christmas is never quite the same after that until some years later when Josie's secret is revealed – at Christmas. William Mayne keeps his secret well-hidden in his perfectly shaped short story.

**72
MORPURGO, Michael**
Colly's Barn
illustrated by Claire Colvin
Heinemann
1991 £2.99 48pp.
0 434 97666 0

Michael Morpurgo's gently written story of how the birds in a barn help each other and, in so doing, save their own home, is expressive and atmospheric. Annie loves the old barn and loves watching Screecher the barn owl and Colly the swift bring up their families in it. But the old barn is about to be pulled down and then where will the birds nest? Annie's close observation of how the birds behave makes absorbing reading.

**73
SEFTON, Catherine**
The Boggart in the Barrel
illustrated by Maureen Bradley
Hamish Hamilton
1991 £4.99 32pp.
0 241 13032 8

Clearing a pile of bricks in the barn, Tom and Suzie come across a sign 'Don't Move The Bricks Around This Barrel or Else'. But Tom and Suzie have already moved the bricks. It is too late. Off flies the lid of the barrel and an angry boggart is released to do his worst. But, several tricks later, it turns out that all the boggart wants is to be loved. Action-packed, this is also a story of tenderness and affection.

74
WADDELL, Martin
Herbie Whistle
illustrated by Anthony Ian
Lewis
Viking
1991 £5.50 80pp.
0 670 83662 1

When Herbie Whistle helps Sammy Dawkins mend the school roof, he doesn't *mean* to leave the bucket drying on the chimney pot but, when the school fills with choking black smoke, Mrs McMaster soon finds that is exactly what has happened. When the school playground becomes full of hopping frogs it doesn't take long to discover that they have hatched from the frogspawn Herbie was meant to take back to the stream above Haddock's Back. Poor Herbie, things always seem to go wrong for him. Martin Waddell's four short stories introduce a delightful and original character against an attractive, old-fashioned setting.

75
WEST, Colin
Monty – up to his neck in
trouble
A. & C. Black
1991 £4.99 64pp.
0 7136 3489 8

Monty, the dog who wears glasses, has a knack of landing himself in trouble. Partly because he is short-sighted and partly because he is incurably nosy, Monty finds himself inviting himself to the wrong birthday party, taking a leading role in a movie and bringing about the end of school custard. In each of the brief episodes that make up this book, Colin West makes serious things funny because of the role Monty plays in them.

76
WILLIAMS, Marcia
Greek Myths for Young
Children
Walker
1991 £9.99 32pp.
0 7445 2101 7

Marcia Williams has rewritten eight Greek myths in a simple and readable way, making them readily accessible to young readers. The briefest of texts is supported by cartoon strip illustrations which give the stories a freshness and immediacy while never taking them too far from their origins.

77
ALCOCK, Vivien
The Dancing Bush
illustrated by Honey De
Lacey
Hamish Hamilton
1991 £4.50 86pp.
0 241 13026 3

The Dancing Bush is a lyrical story, touched with magic. Set in the garden of a country house, it tells of Jed the gardener's boy whose own bush develops into a mysterious, wild green girl who dances in the moonlight with him, acting as the perfect antidote to the spoilt, teasing Annabella, daughter of the landowner. Vivien Alcock's vivid evocation of the garden in the moonlight makes a memorable setting for an enchanting story.

78
ALLEN, Judy
The Long-Loan Llama
illustrated by Kate Aldous
Julia MacRae
1991 £4.99 64pp.
1 85681 060 7

Kate's complete involvement in her local city farm is infectious, drawing readers of *The Long-Loan Llama* into the politics and daily goings on of life on the city farm. Kate is busy looking after the animals, a difficult toddling visitor and the new, long-loan visitor, a llama with some disgusting habits. Her background fears are that the farm is to be taken over by new owners. Judy Allen's observations are sharp and her recognition of children's confusion about things that are obvious to adults is accurate.

79
CAVE, Kathryn
William and the Wolves
illustrated by Stephen
Player
Viking
1991 £6.99 72pp.
0 670 834874

Mary seems to win nothing but indulgence and praise for having an imaginary and invisible lamb whom she totes around with her, so William decides to get his own back by inventing a pack of snarling wolves whom he keeps in the garden shed. But Mary is not easily cowed and William finds inventing increasingly drastic dramas for his wolves becomes an exhausting business. Kathryn Cave has written a witty and clever story around the problems created by an imaginary friend or pet.

80
CRESSWELL, Helen
Posy Bates, Again!
illustrated by Kate Aldous
Bodley Head
1991 £6.99 104pp.
0 370 31592 8

Helen Cresswell creeps right into the skin of Posy Bates, capturing exactly her extraordinary mental contortions which are largely based on unbounded optimism. Posy's conversations with her baby brother Fred are always hilarious. Here she goes even further. In her determination to convince Fred that he will love having a dog around, she leans right into the cot and licks him, just to get him used to the idea. Posy gets her dog who does, of course, lead her into all kinds of fresh disasters. Funny and loving, but never twee, *Posy Bates, Again!* gives a convincing picture of family life.

81
DURANT, Alan
Jake's Magic
illustrated by Duncan
Smith
Walker
1991 £6.99 96pp.
0 7445 2126 2

Told without unnecessary complication or fuss, *Jake's Magic* is a sensitive story about a boy's longing for a cat. The need for a cat is more than just the desire for a pet, having it would satisfy Jake's search for security and his feelings of belonging. Alan Durant's pleasantly low key style makes this story particularly effective.

82
EADINGTON, Joan
Well Done Jonny Briggs!
illustrated by William
Marshall
Hodder & Stoughton
1991 £4.99 76pp.
0 340 53130 4

Without ever preaching or appearing deliberately to be pushing a point, *Well Done Jonny Briggs!* discusses girls playing football with the expectation that they should do so. Joan Eadington's real gift of storytelling, in a slightly old-fashioned style, gives the story of how unlucky Jonny and his friend Pam plan to challenge their swap school to a football match only to discover that they don't allow girls to play in their team, a charming and convincing feel.

83
FINE, Anne
A Sudden Glow of Gold
illustrated by David
Higham
Piccadilly
1991 £5.95 52pp.
1 85340 088 2

Cleverly twisted around familiar genie themes, *A Sudden Glow of Gold* shows the value of Hasan's proverb 'Riches, like camel dung, do no good till they're spread'. Sent upstairs to tidy his bedroom, Toby comes across an old lamp. One rub, and the genie appears. Hasan has been trapped in the lamp for far too long and needs a friend like Toby to wish generously enough to set him free. Anne Fine's light good humour makes an excellent new story in an old tradition.

84
FOREMAN, Michael
The Boy Who Sailed
With Columbus
Pavilion
1991 £9.99 72pp.
1 85145 659 7

Michael Foreman's fictional reconstruction of the story of Columbus and the discovery of the New World is a wonderful story in its own right, as well as giving life to a much celebrated but little known about moment in history. Leif's chance meeting with the great Columbus leads to his employment as ship's boy. Wide-eyed, Leif sets off from Spain on a voyage to a completely New World, where so many things are different. Michael Foreman has created a series of adventures, some linked to reality, which reveal much about how the New World looked to the explorers and some of the problems for both traders and natives. Glorious illustrations accompany the story, making vivid the descriptions in the text.

85
HARRISON, Michael
Trouble in Store
illustrated by David McKee
Andersen
1991 £6.99 92pp.
0 86264 333 3

Michael Harrison tells this detective story at a rattling pace. Reluctantly out shopping with his mum, Matthew is the witness of a nasty piece of shoplifting. And that's just the start of it. When everything starts going wrong at the school raffle, first with the tickets and then with the prizes completely disappearing, Matthew and his friends set about trying to find the thief in their own, slightly unorthodox way. The convincing characters and unpretentious dialogue make the child detective concept plausible and funny.

86
HUSBAND, Tony
WOOD, David
Save the Human!
Hamish Hamilton
1991 £4.99 86pp.
0 241 13137 5

Once upon a time Humans ruled the world. But, because they fought over their world and polluted it, they nearly became extinct and were only preserved by the intervention of animals who protected them and turned them into pets. In this cleverly crafted role-reversal story, Becky Bear begins to question the animals' treatment of humans and, in particular, the morality of some of the experiments practised on them. The obvious message is well carried in this dramatically narrated and fully sustained parable.

87
IRONS, Jane
How To Swap Your
Parents Without Really
Trying
illustrated by Thelma
Lambert
Blackie
1991 £5.95 112pp.
0 216 93114 2

Tom is convinced that his parents are the most boring in the world but, when he has a go at swapping them in a supermarket full of parents, he finds that they are by no means the worst of a bad bunch. Jane Irons' amusing tour of different kinds of families, albeit slightly stereotypical, makes entertaining reading while the reuniting of Tom with his own parents is satisfying and sympathetic.

88
KAYE, Geraldine
The Stone Boy
illustrated by Mei-Yim Low
Heinemann
1991 £3.99 72pp.
0 434 97657 1

Kim's new flat has been carved out of a large old house, formerly used as a Dr Barnardo's home. Kim finds the whole place rather spooky and quickly discovers that her own room is haunted by a little girl struggling to get the cupboard open. Gradually Kim pieces together the story of a tyrannical matron who ruled the home and frightened the children. By finding the key and opening the cupboard Kim sets the unhappy children free and makes Cedar Court a happy place to live. Geraldine Kaye's skill in evoking atmosphere makes this familiar theme into a special story.

89
KING-SMITH, Dick
The Cuckoo Child
illustrated by David
Parkins
Viking
1991 £7.99 110pp.
0 670 83295 2

Dick King-Smith revisits his own previously explored territory in this beautifully constructed and charming story of how a pair of geese come to rear an ostrich. Jack, a farmer's son with a special interest in birds, acquires an ostrich egg on a visit to the local wildlife park. Determined to try and hatch the egg he cunningly, but kindly, tricks the birds into sitting on it for the requisite length of time until the first movements are felt and a large baby ostrich makes its appearance. Dick King-Smith invests all the farmyard animals with clearly defined characters which makes them of interest to human readers without ever detracting from their animal selves.

90
McCALL SMITH,
Alexander
Harriet Bean and the
League of Cheats
illustrated by Jean Baylis
Blackie
1991 £5.95 67pp.
0 216 93085 5

Harriet Bean has some very unusual aunts. Two of them, Aunt Thessalonika and Aunt Japonica run a detective agency. When Harriet gets a call from the aunts she knows that they need her help. Someone is cheating Mr Fetlock. All his horses are losing their races. Disguised as a jockey Harriet determines to solve the mystery and soon finds herself face to face with the League of Cheats. Breathlessly, the adventure hurries along with enough surprise and humour to absorb the attention fully.

91
ROSS, Tony
A Fairy Tale
Andersen
1991 £6.99 32pp.
0 86264 323 6

The illusive quality of magic is subtly explored in Tony Ross's tender and original story of how Bessie unexpectedly finds out about fairies. Bored one afternoon because her books were filled with nonsense about fairies, and with an hour to go till tea, Bessie meets fat old Mrs Leaf from next door. Does Mrs Leaf believe in fairies? Bessie learns how much more there is to magic than she had ever realised as her friendship develops over the years. Set against a pre-war background, *A Fairy Tale* is full of gentle visual surprises which repay careful and repeated visits.

92
TOWNSON, Hazel
Hot Stuff
illustrated by David McKee
Andersen
1991 £5.99 68pp.
0 86264 349 X

Arthur Venger, inventor *extraordinaire*, is determined to find a cure for hot heads. First he invents the specially-formulated potion, next he sets about finding a way of getting people to apply it. Herbie and Kip lend a hand and all three soon become involved in some unexpected adventures. *Hot Stuff* moves at a terrific pace and ends with an excellent surprise.

93
WADDELL, Martin
Little Obie and the Flood
illustrated by Elsie Lennox
Walker
1991 £6.99 79pp.
0 7445 1902 0

The simplicity and directness of Martin Waddell's storytelling gives immediacy to these four brief but dramatic episodes about a young boy, Obie, and the life he leads in the American West. Obie lives in a lonely cabin miles from anywhere, with his grandfather and grandmother. They are lucky to survive the big flood of the title story which washes away many of their neighbours' homes. The flood leaves Obie's friend Marty homelesss and orphaned. Her gradual rehabilitation and Little Obie's understanding of it, makes the central and interlinking theme behind the stories.

94
ALCOCK, Vivien
A Kind of Thief
Methuen
1991 £8.95 196pp.
0 416 15562 6

When Elinor's father is arrested and imprisoned she finds herself having to take responsibility for the family and, most of all, for herself and the secret her father has entrusted to her. Elinor goes to stay with distant relatives and meets Timon whose attitudes make her think about what she has done and the reasons for it. Vivien Alcock tells the story clearly through the eyes of a thirteen-year-old girl showing just how separate from adults the lives, and thinking, of children can be.

95
APPS, Roy
The Secret Summer of Daniel Lyons
Andersen
1991 £6.99 137pp.
0 86264 353 8

Brilliantly set in 1909 against a background of the conflicting strands of Primitive Methodism and the early days of the British Film Industry, *The Secret Summer of Daniel Lyons* is a funny and exciting story, excellently told. Tom Jupe's parents are strict Primitive Methodists. To them, photography is a new-fangled and suspect invention while the South Seas Film Company which arrives in their seaside town is, without doubt, doing the work of the Devil. But Tom's one ambition is to work with the film company. How Tom leads his secret life and how, surprisingly, it leads him back into his father's fold makes fascinating reading.

96
ASHLEY, Bernard
Seeing Off Uncle Jack
illustrated by Kim Harley
Viking
1991 £7.50 80pp.
0 670 83942 6

Skilfully and carefully written, both stylistically and in content, the two stories in *Seeing Off Uncle Jack* are full of tenderness and understanding. Bernard Ashley shows how much can be fitted into a short story and how powerful it can be. In the title story Winnie discovers that the Uncle Jack whom she knew had an unexpected past; an involvement in the black movement which makes her brother Danny reconsider his image of him. 'The Princess Witch' is a lighter weight story, telling of Winnie's slowly learnt lesson that things have a value that is not necessarily related to money.

97
BYARS, Betsy
Bingo Brown, Gypsy
Lover
Bodley Head
1991 £6.99 108pp.
0 370 31553 7

Bingo Brown, the self-doubting hero of two previous novels, finds himself in a shopping mall unable to think what to buy Melissa that could match the amazing present she is promising him; with arms that seem to be growing between breakfast and dinner time; with a girl who is determined that they could become very close. Meanwhile, his parents are having a new baby, a precious brother who may not even make it to *be* a brother. Bingo's view of life, and particularly his conversations with his friends and his parents have a brilliant accuracy, wittily captured in Betsy Byars' enormously readable style.

98
DUNLOP, Eileen
Finn's Island
Blackie
1991 £8.50 128pp.
0 216 93088 X

Although packed almost too full of drama, *Finn's Island* is an excellent adventure story, well-plotted and strong on character. Finn's dream is to return to Hirsay, the remote Hebridean island where his grandfather grew up before it was evacuated. But Finn's vision of life on Hirsay is hopelessly romanticised and it takes a nearly disastrous visit to the island to prove to him that nature can be cruel and to understand that growing up in such an isolated environment can have as many disadvantages as advantages.

99
FORWARD, Toby
The Toad Lady
illustrated by Pat Tayler
Andersen
1991 £6.99 152pp.
0 86264 342 2

Bored at the end of a long summer holiday, George, Steve and Tony are quick to make a mystery out of the fierce lady who told them off for spoiling toadspawn and the young girl who lives with her. Watching through the window, they are sure that the two of them are practising spells. But Tony breaks away from the others and discovers the truth about the girl and what she and the toad lady are doing. After a well-observed but slow start Toby Forward tells a sympathetic story about a boy's gradual understanding of what it might be like to be deaf and his increasing desire to be involved in helping.

100
GIBSON, Andrew
Jemima, Grandma and
the Great Lost Zone
illustrated by Chris Riddell
Faber
1991 £8.99 117pp.
0 571 16455 2

Keeping up a brisk pace, partly through quick repartee, and making witty play of the space setting, Andrew Gibson has written a richly inventive and highly entertaining fantasy. Jemima, Grandma and Birmingham, a likeable but incompetent computer, are sent off on a mission to find out what has happened to part of the universe that seems to have completely disappeared. What follows is a series of encounters with the surprising things that happen in the Great Lost Zone. Despite its science fiction setting, *Jemima, Grandma and the Great Lost Zone* is little concerned with hardware but much concerned with observation of how people behave, and why.

101
GLEITZMAN, Morris
Misery Guts
illustrated by John Levers
Blackie
1991 £7.95 128pp.
1 216 92959 8

The fact that this wholly incredible story is totally compelling is a reflection of Morris Gleitzman's gift for storytelling. Keith's mum and dad have long faces and worried looks. Keith is determined to find a way of cheering them up. Painting their fish and chip shop Tropical Mango fails to do the trick as do all of Keith's other, hare-brained schemes. Somehow Keith finds the perfect answer. Emigration to Paradise, Australia. But will it really be paradise? Keith's search for external ways to find happiness help him to find out more about what it takes to make people happy.

102
HAMILTON, Virginia
Cousins
Gollancz
1991 £9.99 125pp.
0 575 05084 5

The complexities of family relationships are explored to their fullest in this brilliant picture of Cammy and her feelings. Cammy's cousin Patty Ann has everything. Looks, talents, an adoring mother and beautiful clothes. Part of Cammy knows that these are not the things that she wants, but part of her is just plain jealous. Cammy has her brother Andrew, her mom and best of all, her old Gram Tut. She knows the meaning of loving, she is strong and independent. But still she is full of envy and therefore hate of Patty Ann, a feeling so deeply held that when Patty Ann drowns Cammy's sense of guilt is overwhelming. It takes all the family's combined strength to get Cammy through her guilt-ridden grief and to come to terms with it. Virginia Hamilton has written a powerful and compassionate novel that weaves drama and emotion tightly together.

103
HAMLEY, Dennis
The War and Freddy
illustrated by George Buchanan
Andre Deutsch
1991 £4.99 110pp.
0 233 98756 8

The simple style Dennis Hamley has adopted in order to give authenticity to Freddy's storytelling voice, makes this a readily accessible account of the Second World War as it appeared to a child. Freddy was three when the war started. He didn't really understand much about it but there were some things he didn't like – his father going off to be a soldier, for example. Freddy became a 'soldier', too, joining the older boys in his street who had formed a 'home guard'. Their antics and the goings on of the grown-ups, as observed by Freddy, give a strong impression of the unexpected view of the war that many young children must have had.

104
HENDRY, Diana
Harvey Angell
Julia MacRae
1991 £7.99 139pp.
1 85681 061 5

Full of invention and 'atmospheric' in more senses than one, *Harvey Angell* is an original way of telling a poignant story about an unhappy child. Henry lives with his miserable aunt in a house full of elderly lodgers. Aunt Agatha only takes in lodgers who are as quiet and unhappy as herself, until Harvey Angell arrives and somehow hoodwinks Aunt Agatha into renting him the attic. But who is Harvey Angell? Henry's detective work reveals mysterious trips to the graveyard, private conversations in a previously undetected café, 'The Waifs and Strays', and the unorthodox use of a 'connecting kit'. Diana Hendry moves the story along at a good pace while subtly uncovering emotional truths.

105
HILL, Susan
The Glass Angels
illustrated by Valerie
Littlewood
Walker
1991 £9.99 90pp.
0 7445 2120 3

The Glass Angels is a contrived but magical story, rich in atmosphere and subtly understated emotion. Tilly and her mother, living on the small sums made dressmaking, are always struggling to make ends meet. At Christmas time Tilly can't help raising her hopes for something special and wonderful to happen. It even looks as if it might as Tilly's mother works on the beautiful material for Miss Kendall's wedding dress. Even after disaster strikes Tilly goes on believing in miracles. And, something miraculous does happen. Christmas *is* special. Susan Hill tells an old-fashioned story through beautiful prose.

106
McKAY, Hilary
The Exiles
Gollancz
1991 £9.99 191pp.
0 575 04934 0

Hilary McKay's breezy and humorous style combined with her good eye for characters and their interaction, makes *The Exiles* highly readable. Ruth, Naomi, Phoebe and Rachel are dispatched to stay with their larger than life grandmother while their parents spend some newly-inherited money on improving the house. Big Grandma has strong views about everything, particularly about how her granddaughters should behave. Gradually, and reluctantly, the girls adapt to a new way of life and, most importantly, they discover all the things that make Big Grandma so special.

107
MORGAN, Helen
The Witch Doll
Hamish Hamilton
1991 £8.99 142pp.
0 241 13100 6

When Linda frees the wooden doll from the bag it is so tightly tied up in, she doesn't know the evil she is unleashing. But, one look at the doll's face tells her that this is no ordinary doll. The strange and dramatic story of the doll is excellently told by Gran who knows what really happened. Full of period detail, the chilling and gripping story unfolds. Only Linda, if she can screw up the courage, can prevent the logical outcome of the doll's release. Helen Morgan tells a fast-moving and frightening story.

108
PULLEIN-THOMPSON, Christine
The Long Search
Andersen
1991 £6.99 120pp.
0 86264 332 5

Set in any oppressed country where democracy is dead and corruption reigns, *The Long Search* is the story of Ion, struggling to support his dying grandmother in impossible circumstances. With no way out, Ion decides he must find his parents, imprisoned without cause a decade before. Ion's search, his experience of being caught up in the revolution of the moment, his success in finding his parents and the initial problems of their homecoming – all of these are sensitively touched on in this brief but serious novel.

109
RIDLEY, Philip
Krindlekrax
illustrated by Mark Robertson
Cape
1991 £8.99 128pp.
0 224 03149 X

Rich in imagination and invention, *Krindlekrax* is deeply rewarding to read though the self-conscious style is, at times, irritating and

intrusive. The story of Ruskin Splinter who longs to be a hero but being thin, bespectacled and knobbly kneed never gets a chance, being beaten instead by the thug Elvis, is a common enough theme but it is the underground secret of Lizard Street that provides the inspiration and invention of the story. Krindlekrax is a toast-eating monster who lives deep down in the drains under the cracked pavements of Lizard Street. Ruskin proves himself to have the hero qualities he has always wanted when he tames Krindlekrax and, in so doing, breaks free from all of the petty tyrannies that have always surrounded him.

110
WATTS, Marilyn
The Graphicat
Julia MacRae
1991 £7.99 122pp.
0 85681 251 0

Playing a computer game one Friday afternoon, Jo and Tim find the Graphicat is not sticking to the rules. Somehow it frees itself from the game and steps boldly out of the computer. From the beginning it is clear that the Graphicat is no ordinary cat but what its powers are, and how it will use them Jo and Tim still have to find out. Together they try to find the cat and to track down the manufacturer of the disc. Marilyn Watts has woven an excellent adventure around an exciting and imaginative idea.

111
WILLARD, Barbara
The Farmer's Boy
illustrated by Robin Bell Corfield
Julia MacRae
1991 £7.99 100pp.
1 85681 140 9

Harry longs to learn but his days at school are restricted to the few days that it is too wet to farm. Harry's grandfather is a poor tenant farmer, his brothers have scattered to different places, most recently his favourite brother Luke has been deported for poaching deer, so Harry is needed to keep the farm going. But tenant farming is a precarious business and hanging over Harry is the real possibility that Ranger Blagdon will take over his farm. Barbara Willard's delicate observation of the social structure of nineteenth-century England as seen through the eyes of a young lad, give vivid life to a past age.

112
BIERMAN, Valerie
(editor)
No More School?
Methuen
1991 £8.99 127pp.
0 416 15702 5

No More School? is more than just a collection of school stories. The range of experiences, the unusual setting of some of the schools and the interesting introductions that each of the contributors has made to their story gives the genre some fresh dimensions. Alexander McCall Smith tells a ghost story set in a school in Zimbabwe; Vivien Alcock's 'Flowers for the New Girl' also revolves around a ghost, or at least ghostly writing which manages to see off the class bully; Terrance Dicks' 'The Barrier' shows in no uncertain terms why the eleven plus was such a deadly divider. Each in its own way, the nine stories included give insight into an aspect of school life.

113
BERRY, James
The Future Telling Lady
Hamish Hamilton
1991 £8.99 145pp.
0 241 13127 8

In this wide-ranging collection, James Berry shows his understanding of all kinds of people and situations. All of the stories have powerful Jamaican backgrounds and, though the stories are about individuals, many of them also give pictures of the Caribbean way of life. 'Banana-Day Trip' is the story of Boy-Don's terrible homesickness when he goes to stay with his granny. Told humorously and with unfailing insight, it also has a strong background of the busy banana market and how it has been commercialised. 'Mr Mongoose and Mrs Hen' is an allegorical folk tale of the nastiest kind, sharply making its point about corruption. Most powerful of all is the long final story, 'Ajeemah and his Son' which is a cleverly constructed and deeply moving insight into slavery and what it means.

114
BRADMAN, Tony
(editor)
Love Them, Hate Them
Methuen
1991 £8.95 128pp.
0 416 15352 6

Siblings arouse powerful emotions since they provide the main threat to parental affection. The nine stories in this collection explore a range of sibling relationships and their attendant emotions. In 'The Beast' Mick Gowar portrays the incredible anger Mary feels towards her young half-brother; Ann Pilling describes the hostility emanating from Billie when he is first fostered and Robert's wary persistence which breaks it down. Hazel Townson's 'Death by Omelette' shows the extremes to which living with a talented older sister may drive you, while Annie Dalton and Vivien Alcock both write of the devastating effects of an outsider coming between siblings. Sadly, to judge from this collection, it seems to be easier to write of hatred and envy than to explore the strong ties of affection that bind siblings together.

115
CRESSWELL, Helen
Lizzie Dripping and the
Witch
illustrated by Chris Riddell
BBC Books
1991 £8.99
0 563 36210 3

Six new and original stories about Lizzie Dripping and the strange things that happen to her. Even on her own, Lizzie Dripping has an uncanny ability to turn everything upside down. When she is with her witch friend the extraordinary things that happen to Lizzie become more extraordinary than ever. Helen Cresswell takes witches in her stride, making her stories about one thoroughly convincing and wonderfully amusing.

116
FLEETWOOD, Jenni
Happy Birthday
illustrated by Willow
Dent
1991 £7.50 92pp.
0 460 88050 0

The slightly soppy theme of 'birthdays' is, in fact, used to good effect in this collection of inter-related stories about a group of children and the things that happen on their birthdays. Jenni Fleetwood has captured the combination of excitement and anxiety which affects many children and, particularly, Tom's mixed feelings about having a baby sister born right on his birthday.

117
GOWAR, Mick (editor)
Mystery Tour
Bodley Head
1991 £7.99 162pp.
0 370 31579 0

The subtitle 'other stories of detection' is misleading as this is a collection of six amusing and original stories with nothing more than a little unexpected about each. Jan Mark's title story is highly entertaining for the writing and observation though the storyline is rather thin. Much the same is true of Adèle Geras's 'The Peanut Brittle Experience Mystery' which wittily captures the absolute and blind absorption of a teenager in love. In contrast is Joan Aiken's brilliantly contrived and richly imagined fairy story 'The Boy With No Pockets'.

118
GRAHAM, Harriet
Tom's Saturday Trousers
illustrated by Anthony
Lewis
Andre Deutsch
1991 £6.99 116pp.
0 233 98684 7

In the ten short stories about Tom and the kind of things he does Harriet Graham shows insight into how children perceive the world around them and how they make everyday things special. Tom's world revolves around home and school, his parents and his friends. Special things are when it snows which also coincides with the birth of his new sister, the day he finds a lost kitten and the day he runs away from home in a fury. The small print will make these stories hard to read for six-year-olds like Tom, but will still be enjoyable for older children.

119
KLEIN, Robin
Tearaways
Viking
1991 £7.99 133pp.
0 670 83212 X

Ten short stories which show just how nasty children can be, especially to each other. But, this is not a celebration of nastiness. Robin Klein exposes unpleasantness for what it is but she does not necessarily condone it. Often victims get their own back as in the clever and excessive 'Little Beast' and in 'Stone Angel', both caricatures of the meanest kind of school story. 'Elpy' is an elegantly constructed piece of trickery and 'The Key' shows how bad instincts can be tempered by emotion. All Robin Klein's writing has enormous vigour which is reflected in the wide variety of styles which she here adopts.

120
ROSEN, Michael
Clever Cakes
illustrated by Caroline
Holden
Walker
1991 £6.99 96pp.
0 7445 1900 4

Michael Rosen has written seven original and pithy stories which deck out fairy tale morality in new guises. In each, it pays to think quickly and trickily. Cherry-Berry outwits the man who threatens to get the better of her father; the greedy wolf is outwitted by the Clever Cakes in the title story and Flit and Flat cheat the giant Gobbleguts of his dinner. Caroline Holden's illustrations match Michael Rosen's lighthearted wit.

121

Silver Jackanory
BBC Books
1991 £7.99 96pp.
0 563 36171 9

For twenty-five years *Jackanory* has been telling stories to children and this celebratory collection reflects the outstanding quality of those that have been chosen to do the job. In this collection of nine brand new stories there are fresh adventures for favourite characters from Helen Cresswell in 'Lizzie Dripping by Moonlight' and Joan Aiken in 'Arabel's Treehouse'. Dick King-Smith's 'A Narrow Squeak' is a witty mouse story told with all his familiar insights and excellently illustrated by Martin Ursell, while Tony Robinson's 'Skulduggery' is a school story of a most unusual kind. Other contributors include Joan Eadington, Robert Leeson, Nick Wilton, Rory MacGrath, Trevor Neal and Simon Hickson.

122
WYATT, David
(illustrator)
Haunting Christmas
Tales
Scholastic
1991 £7.99 269pp.
0 590 76615 5

Nine original ghostly stories reflecting a wide spread of talents and the full gamut of spooky or unsettling possibilities. Tessa Krailing's 'Jingle Bells' is a domestic affair; a child's unresolved grief over the death of a baby brother who returns, trying to find his way back into the family. Also within the family is Anthony Master's 'The Cracked Smile' in which Ian relives how his mother and sister died and brings peace through the discovery of an old doll. Other stories are more sinister, their spookiness unresolved. Susan Price, Joan Aiken and Robert Swindells are among the contributors.

POETRY

123
AGARD, John
NICHOLS, Grace
No Hickory No Dickory
No Dock
illustrated by Penny Dann
Viking
1991 £7.99 80pp.
0 670 82661 8

A rich blend of nursery rhymes from the Caribbean, *No Hickory No Dickory No Dock* includes traditional rhymes in their Caribbean form alongside contemporary verses by John Agard and Grace Nichols. Together they give a vivid and lively impression of children's play in the Caribbean as well as an insight into how universal and adaptable some favourite rhymes can be.

124
CAUSLEY, Charles
The Young Man of Cury
illustrated by Michael
Foreman
Macmillan
1991 £9.95 110pp.
0 333 53812 9

Michael Foreman has caught exactly the feel of Charles Causley's lyrical, ballad-like poems. Both the small black and white line drawings and the softly-coloured whole page pictures enrich the verses and make the whole book one to savour. Charles Causley has a wonderfully positive view of the world which pervades all his poems. He writes amusingly but always tenderly about many different kinds of people in the opening section 'A Sort of People' and in 'Wise and Foolish'; he captures the feel of the seasons in 'Season and Place', most notably winter in 'Tam Snow'; he weaves magic in 'Magic and Spell' and is, perhaps, at his most charming in 'Song and Story' which includes the title poem 'The Young Man of Cury'.

125
DHONDY, Farrukh
(compiler)
Ranters, Ravers and
Rhymers
Collins
1991 £7.99 160pp.
0 00 191359 X

Subtitled 'Poems by Black and Asian Poets' this is a passionate collection which demands dedicated reading and offers enormous rewards in terms of comprehension of some of the feelings of those whom Farrukh Dhondy describes as 'Black British'. Some of the poems are about 'home', some about Britain and how it feels to live here as an outsider, and some like Grace Nichols' 'With Apologies to Hamlet' are about other things altogether. The overall tone of the collection, however, is determinedly hard hitting, making strong and profoundly moving statements whether about domestic politics as in Lorna Goodison's 'For My Mother' (May I Inherit Half Her Strength) or national politics as in Mahmood Jamal's 'A Peasant in Bengal'.

126
EDWARDS, Richard
The House That Caught a
Cold
illustrated by Sarah Jane
Stewart
Viking
1991 £7.50 78pp.
0 670 83583 8

From the title poem onwards, most of the poems in this collection have a lighthearted exuberance which makes them instantly engaging. Richard Edwards has a strong sense of rhythm, which makes the verses easy to read, and a delight in juxtaposing contrasting images which often gives a quirky humour. 'One Wet Day' starts with quite ordinary Jackie and Jimmy picking a strawberry and lettuce respectively but it ends with Zuleika setting off to track panthers. 'Daniel and the Lions' tells of how the six lions on Daniel's lampshade come alive at night.

127
FOSTER, John
Four O'Clock Friday
Illustrated by Debbie Cook
Oxford
1991 £2.95 64pp.
0 19 276093 9 **P**

John Foster's sharp eye has caught exactly how children view school, parents, siblings, friends and much more besides. His sharp ear has caught children's language enabling him to write poems that speak directly to them. Although mostly lighthearted, some of the best poems in the collection reflects the unhappiness of children at times such as when a family breaks up. 'There are four chairs round the table' is poignant without becoming mawkish. 'There are four chairs round the table,/Where we sit down for our tea./But now we only set places/For Mum, for Terry and me'. Closely grouped in themes which gives it a bit of shape, this is an exceptionally enjoyable collection.

128
FOSTER, John
(compiler)
Twinkle Twinkle
Chocolate Bar
Oxford
1991 £10.95 102pp.
0 19 276092 0

Stuffed full of new poems which are readily accessible to the very youngest listeners, this is a refreshing and exciting collection. John Foster has selected poems that explore everyday experiences in an amusing or interesting way. They have the qualities of nursery rhymes but with a contemporary feel. The use of different illustrators for different spreads endorses the range of emotions captured in the poems and adds an attractive visual brightness to an already verbally vibrant collection.

129
HARRISON, Michael
(compiler)
STUART-CLARKE,
Christopher (compiler)
A Year Full of Poems
Oxford
1991 £9.95 140pp.
0 19 276097 1

Carefully ordered into the months of the year which makes it extremely easy to use, this is nonetheless an immensely varied collection of poems. The selectors have chosen broadly from both old and new poets, giving a range of interpretations to each theme. March, for example, includes a view of Spring from both Wordsworth and Adrian Henri. Funny poems, serious poems, all have been selected to appeal to readers of eight or more.

130
HARVEY, Anne
(compiler)
Shades of Green
illustrated by John
Lawrence
Julia MacRae
1991 £14.99 192pp.
1 85681 031 3

The beautiful and thoughtful production of *Shades of Green* makes it a tempting book to read from. It sets a mood which is well matched by the poems. These have been skilfully selected to reflect the 'green spirit' and have been grouped under headings such as 'A Green Hope', 'Goodbye to Hedges' and 'Bird-World, Leaf-Life'. Anne Harvey has chosen poems, old and new, from all over the world to illustrate her theme. All encourage the conservation of nature and our environment in different ways. But, although the book has a specific message to impart, it never seems to preach. Instead it stands as a glorious celebration of nature and how much it offers us to appreciate.

131
HUTH, Angela
(compiler)
Casting a Spell
illustrated by Jane Ray
Orchard
1991 £9.99 96pp.
1 85213 290 6

An anthology of new poems written specially for children is a treat indeed. Like all the best poems for children they are by no means all childish including as they do George Mackay Brown's 'Our Pier: Orkney' which gives a perfect, tiny portrait of the individuals in a small, local community and Sue Townsend's black 'A Warning to Cat Owners' which pulls no punches about what happens to cats because they don't know the highway code. Richard Edwards, Roy Fuller, Max Fatchen, Wes Magee and Wendy Cope with her sharp, accurate older child's view of 'The Baby of the Family' are among the other contributors.

132
McGOUGH, Roger
You At the Back
Cape
1991 £8.99 128pp.
0 224 03111 2

This, the second collection of McGough's poetry spanning the years 1967-1987, shows his enormous versatility as well as his huge delight in all kinds of poetry. Though sometimes topical as in 'Poem for the opening of Christ the King Cathedral, Liverpool', most of the poems have a timelessness because they reflect a mood or a moment which can happen to anyone anywhere. Typical of McGough's writing is 'Vegetarians', a hugely funny poem that also carries a thought-provoking message: 'Vegetarians are cruel, unthinking people./Everybody knows that a carrot screams when grated./That a peach bleeds when torn apart.'

133
NICHOLS, Grace
(compiler)
Can I Buy A Slice of Sky?
illustrated by Liz Thomas
Blackie
1991 £8.95 112pp.
0 216 93090 1

From its wonderful title on, *Can I buy A Slice of Sky?* is a poetry book to relish. Grace Nichols has chosen poems from Black, Asian and American Indian backgrounds all of which have a clear cultural identity while also speaking directly to children everywhere. Divided into eight sections under headings such as 'My Kind of School', 'The Reasons I Like Chocolate' and 'Grown-Up Blues . . . Children Blues', the anthology covers a vast range of subjects. Some are domestic as in one of Grace Nichols' own contributions, 'Granny Granny Please Comb My Hair', which sums up exactly the special part grandparents can play in a child's life, and some are political like 'Speak', a poem from Pakistan on the importance of free speech. Liz Thomas's illustrations, like the poems themselves, make their points boldly but lightly.

134
PATTEN, Brian (editor)
The Puffin Book of
Twentieth-Century
Children's Verse
illustrated by Michael
Foreman
Viking
1991 £12.99 414pp.
0 670 81475 X
Puffin
1991 £5.99 414pp.
0 14 032236 1 **P**

Arranged in a reverse chronological order, this collection of twentieth-century poetry can be read as an unravelling of a long and strong tradition of poetry for children. Brian Patten has selected some of the best poems written specially for children by contemporary poets such as John Agard, Michael Rosen, himself, Allan Ahlberg, Jack Prelutsky, Roger McGough and Charles Causley (and there are many more, too numerous to mention); some poems written specially for children by now dead poets such as A.A. Milne, Eleanor Farjeon, Stevie Smith, Walter De La Mare and Rudyard Kipling; and some poems written for adults but which may readily be enjoyed by children such as Robert Frost's 'Stopping by Woods on a Snowy Evening', W.H. Auden's 'The Night Mail' and Edward Thomas's 'Adlestrop'. The selection has been so careful that each poem is a gem and the whole provides as tempting a taster as possible for the rich world of poetry that lies beyond its covers.

135
PRELUTSKY, Jack
Something BIG Has Been
Here
illustrated by James
Stevenson
Heinemann
1991 £10.99 160pp.
0 434 95738 0

Jack Prelutsky is always witty and rarely unkind. His poems are endlessly inventive about people, animals and situations. 'My frog is a frog that is hopelessly hoarse,/my frog is a frog with a reason, of course,/my frog is a frog that cannot croak a note,/my frog is a frog with a frog in its throat.' A typical Prelutsky poem. Easy to read and remember and perfectly illustrated by James Stevenson.

136
ROSEN, Michael
(compiler)
A World of Poetry
illustrated by Larry Wilkes
Kingfisher
1991 £9.95 256pp.
0 86272 550 X

A World of Poetry is a substantial collection of poems which reflects the enormous range of content and styles embraced under the umbrella of poetry. Michael Rosen has selected cleverly for a clever title including poems which fall within the scope of the geographical world as well as the world of ideas and feelings. Mixing classical and contemporary verse enables readers to savour the best poetry of all times and to enjoy the different styles of different periods.

137
SCANNELL, Vernon
Travelling Light
illustrated by Tony Ross
Bodley Head
1991 £7.99 64pp.
0 370 31581 2

Devoted to travelling – by car, rickshaw, elephant – or almost any other method you can think of, this is a witty and varied collection of poems which will be readily enjoyed by eight-year-olds and over. Vernon Scannell pinpoints details such as idiotic car stickers in 'Stickers', while capturing the mood of cycling in 'Uphill' and the spirit of boating in 'Beauty of Boats'.

138
WATSON, Carol
(compiler)
Prayers for a Fragile
World
illustrated by Rhian Nest
James
Lion
1991 £6.99 93pp.
0 7459 1949 9

Taken from a wide range of sources including children's own writing, *Prayers for a Fragile World* is a well-selected collection of prayers and poems concerned with a wide range of important contemporary issues such as the environment and how we treat it, and social injustice and what might be done about it. Neatly divided into sections such as 'Thank you, Lord', 'Lord, teach us to care', and 'Lord, in the future', this is a useful and powerful tool for discussing particular issues.

139
WILSON, Raymond
To Be A Ghost
illustrated by Alan Rowe
Viking
1991 £7.99 109pp.
0 670 83695 8

Ghosts, witches, mysterious tappings at windows – all of these are included in Raymond Wilson's amusing and atmospheric collection of poems devoted, mostly lightheartedly, to magic, mystery and the supernatural. Rarely chilling, Raymond Wilson instead brings enormous zest and vigour to his spooky subjects making them seem almost alive even to the most hardened sceptics.

140
CHRISP, Peter
The Roman Empire
Wayland
1991 £8.50 48pp.
0 7502 0199 1

From the growth of Rome and the spread of its influence, to the last days of the empire and the legacy it left behind, this is a thorough study of all aspects of an exceptionally influential culture and government. Peter Chrisp describes details of an ordinary Roman's way of life and explains why so much of what we do today has been shaped by, among other things, Roman laws, language and architecture.

141
CONNOLLY, Peter
The Roman Fort
Oxford
1991 £5.95 32pp.
0 19 917108 4

Written as exciting narrative, *The Roman Fort* makes the life of a Roman soldier into a good story. Based on a Roman fort on Hadrian's Wall Peter Connolly tells how the soldiers lived, what particular jobs they did and what threats they were under as they struggled to impose Roman rule on Britain.

142
CUMMING, David
Spain
Wayland
1991 £6.95 32pp.
1 85210 967 X

Spanish children give snippets of information about their lives which, taken together, build up into a portrait of Spanish society in all its diversity. Farming, industry, sports and pastimes, school and transport are just some of the topics brought to life through the chatty text and attractive photographs.

143
DEFRATES, Joanna
What Do We Know About the Egyptians?
Simon & Schuster Young Books
1991 £8.99 48pp.
0 7500 0853 9

Posed as a series of questions, each of the double-page spreads in *What Do We Know About the Egyptians?* looks at an aspect of the Egyptian way of life. The emphasis is on the domestic, with subjects such as 'Did Egyptians Have Families Like Ours?', 'What Did the Egyptians Do on their Holidays?' and 'What Did the Egyptians Wear?' Political and religious issues are not neglected and all the information is given in brief but clear passages. Illustrations and photographs are excellently used to match the text.

144
FYSON, Nance
Rich World Poor World
Oxford
1991 £9.95 88pp.
0 19 913321 2

Both the contrasts that separate and the links that join the different countries of the world are examined in *Rich World Poor World*. The effect of extreme poverty on Mali and other drought-ridden countries and the reasons for it are juxtaposed with the relative wealth of newly industrialised countries such as Hong Kong. Energy, health, population, trade and the environment around the world are just some of the subjects tackled in this issue-led book. Photographs, cartoons and diagrams complement the text well.

145
MACDONALD, Fiona
A Medieval Cathedral
illustrated by John James
Simon & Schuster Young Books
1991 £7.99 48pp.
0 7500 0787 7

Excellent detail, both in text and illustration, gives an accurate impression of the thought behind and work that went into building a medieval cathedral. Without labouring the point, Fiona Macdonald shows how skilled the craftsmen were, managing as they did without the use of technologies which we nowadays take for granted. But, the book is not only about the building of the cathedral. It is also about the people who used it, the clergy – their beliefs and their relationships with the landlords, and the congregation of peasants for whom the cathedral was more than just a place of worship.

146
MORLEY, Jacqueline
BERGIN, Mark
JAMES, John
An Egyptian Pyramid
Simon & Schuster Young Books
1991 £8.99 48pp.
0 7500 0771 0

Every detail of a pyramid – its building, its meaning and its relationship with the rest of Egyptian life – is fully described in this 'Inside Story'. The text is divided into different aspects of the process, allowing room to cover such details as the daily rations for the workers and information about a strike. But this is more than just an account of the pyramid. It is also a comprehensive introduction to Egyptian society.

147
POSTGATE, Oliver
LINNELL, Naomi
Columbus
Kingfisher
1991 £7.95 48pp.
0 86272 738 3

Subtitled 'The Triumphant Failure', this is a wonderfully readable account of what Columbus set out to do, how he failed, and what he achieved instead. Typical of his period, Columbus was sure that he was protected by God in his daring and dangerous explorations. Certainly he was extremely lucky that he stayed alive as, having at last raised the money for the trip, he set off with his ships *Pinta, Nina* and the *Santa Maria* in an attempt to find Japan. The story of the different journeys is briskly and seriously told while the illustrations add some amusing extra details.

148
ROSS, Stewart
Food We Ate
Wayland
1991 £6.50 32pp.
0 7502 0144 4

Looking back at the food of the past tells far more about people than just what they ate. What foods were available and why, how food was prepared and by whom, what the shops sold and how families ate meals – all of these are illustrated in contemporary photographs which make their points clearly. The text provides useful background information and detail.

149
SAUNDERS, Pete
What It's Like To Be Old
Franklin Watts
1991 £6.99 32pp.
0 7496 9634 7

Pete Saunders discusses old age from the point of view of the very young. He looks at what young people can give to the elderly in terms of practical support as well as what the young can get from the old through conversation and, in particular, the special relationship of grandparents to their grandchildren. The overall message is a very positive one without being at all sentimental or underestimating the problems of old age.

150
BAILEY, Donna
Wasting Water
Franklin Watts
1991 £6.99 32pp.
0 7496 0482 4

Why it is important to save water and some sensible practical ways of doing so are well described in *Wasting Water*. How we get water and save it and the many different ways we use it around the world is shown in photographs and diagrams as well as in the text. A good glossary explains the more technical terms.

151
CHINERY, Michael
Wild World of Animals:
Deserts
illustrated by David Wright
Kingfisher
1991 £4.95 40pp.
0 86272 725 1

David Wright's precise and finely drawn illustrations capture the feel of the desert and the interaction of the wildlife that lives in it as well as describing the habits of individual animals, birds and insects in detail. The jumping jerboa, the pack rat, the dancing scorpion and the Arabian camel are just some of the animals included. 'Fact' boxes supply snippets of information not included in the text and 'Survival Watch' boxes show what dangers surround the different animals and why.

152
COSGROVE, Brian
Weather
Dorling Kindersley
1991 £7.99 68pp.
0 86318 578 9

The beautiful presentation of this 'Eyewitness' guide makes absorbing the information it offers a treat. The science of weather patterns and weather forcasting underlies the more detailed study of more particular conditions – A Sunny Day, The Birth of a Cloud, Thunder and Lightning and Wind, among them. Most of the information comes from extended picture captions which, well-reinforced visually, explain exactly what is happening.

153
CROSS, Graham
The Fascinating World of
Ants
*Simon & Schuster Young
Books*
1991 £5.99 32pp.
0 7500 0954 3

Graphic illustrations show ants at work, building their homes, nesting, feeding, travelling and fighting off their enemies. Much is shown in cross section which has the effect of apparently taking the reader right into the ant's world. The text is detailed but clear, making its information interesting and comprehensible.

154
JENNINGS, Terry
PARKER, Steve
PARKER, Jane
Territories
Franklin Watts
1991 £7.99 32pp.
0 7496 0694 0

All animals, insects, birds and fish have territories which they mark out and defend in a variety of ways. Territories are important for survival sometimes because food is scarce and sometimes because protection is needed from predators. Individual territory, group territory, the marking of territory and the fights to preserve it are all covered in this wide-ranging introduction to the subject.

155
KELLY, Janet
Create Your Own Nature Reserve
Simon & Schuster Young Books
1991 £7.99 46pp.
0 7500 0841 5

Packed full of information and practical advice, *Create Your Own Nature Reserve* shows exactly how to make all kinds of habitats and how to look after them. A woodland habitat, a wetland habitat, a logpile habitat – each has its own flora and fauna and attracts its own wildlife. Designed to encourage children to become more closely involved in nature it shows how much there is to see wherever you live.

156
KNAPP, Brian
Grasslands
Simon & Schuster Young Books
1991 £8.99 48pp.
0 7500 0860 1

An excellent guide to a single and important part of the environment, *Grasslands* describes the physical geography of different kinds of grasslands and then discusses the contribution man has made to both their development and destruction. The text is detailed with additional information contained in the captions to the clear diagrams and photographs.

157
LEMMON, Tess
Monkeys
Wayland
1991 £6.95 32pp.
0 7502 0030 8

In a series 'Wildlife At Risk' *Monkeys* first shows just how many different kinds of monkeys there are and how they live in the wild, and then describes graphically, but not over-sensationally, the threat that they are under from the destruction of the rain forest and from the long-standing tradition of keeping monkeys as pets and as performers. Practical advice on how to take individual action to preserve monkeys is also given.

158
McCARTHY, Colin
Reptile
Dorling Kindersley
1991 £7.99 64pp.
0 86318 576 2

Every scrap of information about reptiles and how they live is shown in close (some almost too close for comfort) photographic detail. The wealth of facts included here is spectacular, covering all aspects of a variety of reptile habits and habitats. The information is mostly given as captions to details of the photographs which makes it vivid and easy to understand.

159
PALMER, Joy
Oceans
Franklin Watts
1991 £6.99 32pp.
0 7496 0572 3

This is an interesting and sound 'First Start' look at oceans – what they are, where they are, what lives in them, what minerals come from them and what threats there are to them. Each aspect is covered in a well laid out double-page spread which has a brief text and good supporting illustrations.

160
POWELL, Jillian
Jumpers
Firefly
1991 £4.95 24pp.
1 85485 102 0

From leaf hoppers to people, with all kinds of animals in between, *Jumpers* shows how different creatures jump. The action is shown in photographs matched by a simple text which explains briefly why each of the animals jumps and which parts of the body they use when doing so.

161
WATTS, Barrie
24 Hours in a Desert
Franklin Watts
1991 £8.95 46pp.
0 7496 0540 5

Brilliant close-up photography shows the animals, insects and plants of the desert during different times of day. In the desert the temperature variations throughout the day are significant, which has a profound effect on the behaviour of all the wildlife. Barrie Watts' text is vivid, bringing all aspects of an extraordinary habitat and the creatures in it sharply into focus.

162
WATTS, Barrie
Stick Insects
Franklin Watts
1991 £6.50 32pp.
0 7496 0604 5

Everything you need to know about keeping stick insects is shown in the attractive photographs and brief text of this recent addition to the 'Keeping Minibeasts' series. Stick insects are relatively easy to look after which makes them good, if not dramatic, pets to keep.

163
BARDON, Keith
Exploring Forces and
Structures
illustrated by Marilyn Clay
Wayland
1991 £7.95 48pp.
0 7502 0001 4

'Floating and Sinking', 'Gravity', 'Flying High' and 'Surface Tension' are just some of the forces which are described in this detailed study. The science behind each force and how it can be used or harnessed is described in the text and then reinforced through the accompanying experiments which demonstrate each of the principles.

164
BENDER, Lionel
Invention
Dorling Kindersley
1991 £7.99 64pp.
0 86318 577 0

The clear definition of an invention as 'something that was devised by human effort and that did not exist before' launches *Invention* which then follows with a chronological arrangement of lucid accounts of some of the most important inventions from 'Tools' and 'the Wheel' to 'Plastics' and 'the Silicon Chip'. How and why a particular invention occurred and how it has been usefully harnessed is all explained in the text and in the extended captions which accompany the excellent illustrations.

165
BROWN, David J.
The Kingfisher Book of
How They Were Built
Kingfisher
1991 £9.95 144pp.
0 86272 760 X

Covering much more than just the design and construction of buildings through the ages, this is a guide to civilisation through buildings. Divided into 'The Ancient World,' 'The Age of Discovery', 'The "New" Technology' and 'The Modern World' this shows how simple shelters, public buildings and structures such as bridges were built. What materials were used, what technologies were available, why certain buildings were built when they were, all are covered in the text which is fully illustrated with plans, diagrams, cross-sections and pictures of work in progress.

166
DAVIES, Kay
OLDFIELD, Wendy
Hot and Cold
Wayland
1991 £6.50 32pp.
0 7502 0205 X

A first introduction to temperature changes, their effects and their causes, *Hot and Cold* asks some simple questions and gives some good examples of experiments which show temperature changes in everyday situations.

167
DUNN, Andrew
Lifting by Levers
illustrated by E.D. Carr
Wayland
1991 £6.95 32pp.
0 7502 0218 1

An excellent, clearly and lightly explained account of how levers work and how essential they are in so many everyday activities. Andrew Dunn divides the levers up into categories showing the slight variations there are between different kinds of levers and what they do. E.D. Carr's illustrations give this picture book a quality which makes the subject especially approachable.

168
HANN, Judith
How Science Works
Dorling Kindersley
1991 £12.99 192pp.
0 86318 602 5

Judith Hann shows that science is all around us as part of our daily life. It is not confined to school or a laboratory but can easily be explored at home with ordinary, non-scientific equipment. She also shows that science is creative and fun. Divided into six distinct sections: 'The World of Matter,' 'Energy, Force and Motion', 'Light and Sound', 'Air and Water', 'Electricity and Magnetism' and 'Electronics and Computers' *How Science Works* covers an enormous amount of ground through a clear text and outstanding illustrations which attract immediate attention.

169
HULL, Robert (editor)
Science Poetry
illustrated by Annabel
Spenceley
Wayland
1991 £7.95 46pp.
0 7502 0223 8

To use science as inspiration for poetry is innovative and highly successful. Robert Hull has quite rightly interpreted 'science' as widely as possible so that he may include seven-year old Ryan Goad's poem 'Bubbles' and Katherine Gallagher's 'Song for an Unborn' alongside Ogden Nash's witty poem about Professor Twist, 'The Purist'. Together these poems show how the deep forces of science are inspiring to speculation and humour.

170
LAMBERT, Mark
Food Technology
Wayland
1991 £7.95 46pp.
0 7502 0005 7

Seeing the processes behind the production of food is enough to put one off eating, but it is also important to know how the food we eat has been treated. The recent technologies of fast freezing and fast cooking with a microwave have dramatically changed not only what food is eaten but also how food is prepared and with that come changes in traditional domestic roles. Mark Lambert gives a lot of scientific background to modern food technology covering every aspect from the way the basic ingredients are farmed through to how they are eventually sold and prepared in the home.

171
McTAVISH, Douglas
Joseph Lister
Wayland
1991 £7.99 48pp.
0 7502 0168 1

Telling the story of the life of Joseph Lister is an excellent way of exploring some of the most important medical breakthroughs of the last 150 years. When Lister trained as a medical student hospitals were dirty and overcrowded and operations were both excruciatingly painful and highly dangerous as the risk of infection was ever present. Lister recognised the need for clean hospitals and the vital importance of antiseptic conditions when operating. With the introduction of these, all kinds of new surgical techniques became possible and are practised today. Douglas McTavish brings insight to Lister himself and to the work he did, setting it soundly in its historical context.

172
OLLERENSHAW, Chris
TRIGGS, Pat
Wind-Ups
A. & C. Black
1991 £5.99 32pp.
0 7136 3357 3

Wind-Ups is a first book about energy using toys to demonstrate particular scientific principles. Stretching and springing, bouncing, winding things up and using gravity are all shown in practice in the clear colour photographs. The harnessing of energy both naturally and by man is well explained in the text.

173
PARKER, Steve
History of Medicine
Belitha
1991 £8.95 64pp.
1 85561 057 4

This chronological study of medicine is full of information about good health and bad, medicines for the prevention of disease and for curing disease, and speculation about what health is and what the medicines of the future might be. A book of breadth rather than depth, this is an interesting and informative introduction to how medicine has developed.

174
PLUCKROSE, Henry
Machines
photographs by Chris
Fairclough
Franklin Watts
1991 £6.99 32pp.
0 7496 0660 6

This is a photographic introduction to machines, what they do and why, with a text that explains the most basic principles. Domestic appliances such as mixers, vacuum cleaners and hairdriers are given prominence among more dramatic machines such as aeroplanes, power saws and incubators. *Machines* makes a good base for asking questions about how machines work and what jobs they can do.

175
ROWAN, Peter
The Amazing Voyage of
the Cucumber Sandwich
illustrated by Polly Noakes
Cape
1991 £6.99 96pp.
0 224 03113 9

Peter Rowan's 'story in three parts, set in the human body' tells exactly, and graphically, what happens to a cucumber sandwich when it is eaten. The function of different kinds of food, how it is physically changed on its journey, what happens to it chemically and what the different organs of the body do are all chattily described within the story.

176
TAYLOR, Kim
Water
Belitha
1991 £6.95 32pp.
1 85561 077 9

The many aspects of water, one of the Earth's most important natural resources, are shown through photographs, experiments and brief, factual accounts. The presentation looks confusing but the information provided fits together well and gives an overall coherent picture.

177
TWIST, Clint
Energy Sources
Wayland
1991 £7.95 48pp.
0 7502 0067 7

'Coal', 'Oil and Gas', 'Nuclear Power', 'Solar Energy', 'Energy from the Elements' – under these broad headings Clint Twist takes a detailed look at the major sources of energy in the world, how they are harnessed and how they are used. His accounts are predominantly factual but they also include an element of value judgement about particular energy sources. Photographs and diagrams accompany the text and there is a useful glossary.

178
WILLIAMS, John
Electricity
Wayland
1991 £6.50 32pp.
0 7502 0169 X

With a strong emphasis on practical experiments *Electricity* shows the different parts of an electric circuit and the different ways in which electricity can be used. Bulbs and batteries, switches, making a circuit, conductors, messages, magnets and printed circuits – all of these are clearly described with accompanying practical experiments.

179
ALLEN, Bob
Mountain Biking
Wayland
1991 £7.95 48pp.
0 7502 0182 7

Biking, once a rather tame activity, has been turned into something fast, furious and glamorous with the arrival of the mountain bike. Dramatic photographs and a punchy text show how much skill, stamina and practice is needed to become a serious, competitive rider.

180
BRAND, Jill
SHORT, Caroline
The Green Umbrella
illustrated by Jane Ray
A. & C. Black
1991 £8.50 106pp.
0 7136 3390 5

A wonderful resource, *The Green Umbrella* is packed full of stories, songs, poems, fact boxes and activities which stimulate thought on environmental issues. The material comes from all over the world, reflecting particular concerns and also the global extent of anxiety about the environment. Some of the most thought-provoking material has been written by children themselves.

181
DEVONSHIRE, Hilary
Water
Franklin Watts
1991 £7.99 32pp.
0 7496 0534 0

Subtitled 'Science Through Art', *Water* is an excellent introduction to the many forms water can take and, in particular, the central role it plays in both science and art. Clear photographs show all the different things that can be done with water – diluting to make water colours, evaporating to make crystals, freezing to make solids. The text describes the processes in detail and the scientific principles behind them.

182
JACKMAN, Wayne
My Book About the Body
Wayland
1991 £6.50 24pp.
0 7502 0121 5

A first guide to the body and what it can do. Wayne Jackman's simple text accompanies bold, bright photographs which stimulate discussion about the way the body works, how it must be looked after and the ways in which we differ from each other.

183
LIM, Jessie
Exploring Chinese Food
Mantra
1991 £7.95 32pp.
0 947679 91 X

The diversity of Chinese food, the particular significance of different dishes and an account of where some of the ingredients come from and how they are harvested make up this mouth-watering and informative guide. The beautiful presentation of Chinese food allows the text to be accompanied by attractive and tempting photographs.

184
O'REILLY, Susie
Textiles
illustrated by Jenny
Hughes
Wayland
1991 £7.95 48pp.
0 7502 0040 5

A detailed introduction to textiles, running through the different types of textiles, how they are made, what they can be made into, how to dye them and what designs to use on them. Practical activities are explained, showing just how much textile work can be done on a domestic scale and with materials that are ready to hand.

185
PARKER, Steve
Singing a Song
Franklin Watts
1991 £7.99 32pp.
0 7496 0620 7

Singing a song uses a surprising number of different parts of your body. Photographs and diagrams show the internal and external effects while the text describes the complicated stages that are gone through from the moment of thinking about making a sound to actually producing one. *Singing a Song* makes the process interesting and easy to understand. Further scientific weight is added by the accompanying experiments which show the principles behind the practice.

186
SANDELSON, Robert
Ice Sports
Wayland
1991 £7.50 48pp.
0 7502 0231 9

The Winter Olympics have never had the same prestige as the Summer Olympics but, gradually, things are changing as all kinds of winter sports gain in popularity. Robert Sandelson gives a brief history of each of the different sports and tells the life stories of some of their most famous exponents. Vigorous photographs show just how competitive these sports have become.

187
THOMSON, Ruth
The Book of the Seasons
photographs by Ruth
Millard
Franklin Watts
1991 £9.95 126pp.
0 7496 0225 2

Imaginative craft ideas for all seasons form the basis for this attractively presented book. Making things out of what is available or seasonally appropriate includes a Spring section on how to make an enormous range of coloured eggs, making nests and baskets and making sophisticated paper cuttings. 'Summer' shows how to dry flowers and make fragrant bags and shell pictures. On a larger scale, 'Autumn' shows how to make a beautiful nature house hung with seeds and berries. Photographs make vivid the finished products and are also used to provide useful background scientific information.

188
WOOD, Tim
Racing Drivers
Wayland
1991 £6.95 32pp.
0 7502 0109 6

In a series called 'Living Dangerously' *Racing Drivers* is largely made up of dramatic photographs showing racing drivers and their cars in a variety of desperate positions. Tim Wood's text stresses how much skill is needed to be a racing driver, the competitive nature of racing and also captures the glamour associated with it.

189
WRIGHT, Rachel
Knights
Franklin Watts
1991 £7.99 32pp.
0 4796 0699 1

Though designed as a craft topic *Knights* is also full of information about the history of knights and how they lived. Rachel Wright's enthusiasm for her subject brings the history alive and matches it well with craft topics making brass rubbings, helmets, stained glass windows and even a complete castle. There is an excellent glossary and list of further reading for those whose imagination is captured.

190
ELLIOTT, Michele
Feeling Happy Feeling Safe
illustrated by Alice Englander
Hodder & Stoughton
1991 £6.95 32pp.
0 340 54664 6
Hodder & Stoughton
1991 £3.99 32pp.
0 340 55386 5 **P**

Telling children about potential dangers without frightening them too much is an important but difficult task. Michele Elliott uses a picture book format in this safety guide for young children. Four friends – Mike, Emma, James and Anne – do everyday activities like playing in the playground and shopping, they know what it is like to have a babysitter and to be addressed by a stranger. Most importantly they know who to talk to when things go wrong or if something happens that they don't like. Best to be used with children rather than for children on their own, *Feeling Happy Feeling Safe* raises important issues and discusses them in a sensible and reassuring way.

REFERENCE

191
ADAMS, Simon
BRIQUEBEC, John
KRAMER, Ann
Illustrated Atlas of World
History
Kingfisher
1991 £10.95 160pp.
0 86272 761 8

History told through Geography may best describe the thinking behind this Atlas. Divided into four sections it shows how different societies have developed. 'The Ancient World' looks at the very first people that have been traced and how they learned to use tools, to trade, to build and to worship. 'Trade and Religion' explores the period from 450 AD with the spread of organised religions, the development of empires with its inherent threat of invasions, and the growth of trade. 'Exploration and Empire' covers the three hundred year span from 1450-1750 while the final section 'Revolution and Technology' examines societies in upheaval and under new pressures with the emergence of new technologies. The text is both readable and coherent, exploring unproven theories as well as offering pure information. Excellent illustrations and the widespread use of maps makes this a rich source of visual information as well.

192
CARWARDINE, Mark
The Animal Atlas
Oxford
1991 £7.95 68pp.
0 19 831685 2

Grouping animals together according to where they live gives a clear picture of individual species as well as telling plenty about how different animals interact and depend upon one another. Mark Carwardine has condensed an enormous amount of information into short, highly readable entries describing the habits and behaviour of animals all over the world.

193
The Dorling Kindersley
Children's Illustrated
Encyclopedia
Dorling Kindersley
1991 £25.00 645pp.
0 86318 629 7

The information presented in this highly illustrated encyclopedia is a rich mixture reflected by a run of entries such as 'Sir Winston Churchill', 'Circuses', and 'Cities'. Subjects are discussed on a whole page which is broken up into sections or, occasionally, where the overall heading encompasses a particularly large range of material, on a double-page spread. The style is discursive and the illustration tends more towards picture than diagram making this an attractive book to read as well as a valuable source of information.

194
Kingfisher Science Encyclopedia
Kingfisher
1991 £24.95 780pp.
0 86272 697 2

Interpreting science in the very broadest sense, this is a wide-ranging encyclopedia which presents information in a clear and readable way while encouraging wide reading through its easy to use cross-referencing system. There are almost 1000 entries which include scientific principles such as 'Diffraction' and 'Diffusion', points for discussion such as the entries on 'Instinct' and 'Pollution', and pure fact as in the entry on 'Teeth'. The entries are well-illustrated and often include simple, practical experiments to prove their points.

195
Our Planet Earth
Moonlight
1991 £9.99 78pp.
1 85103 128 6

Our Planet Earth is volume 1 in a series of 'First Encyclopedias' which are designed to create a whole picture of a subject from a number of separate entries. The subjects are linked thematically rather than alphabetically and are divided into sections – 'The Solar System', 'The Galaxies', 'Around the Earth', 'The Life of the Earth' and 'The Shaping of the Earth'. Large type and very simple entries in short sentences make this a useful factfinder for the very young while the illustrations provide the basis for further discussion.

196
Oxford Children's Encyclopedia
Oxford
1991 £125 7 volumes
0 19 910139 6

The Oxford Children's Encyclopedia is a comprehensive reference source contained in six volumes and a good index volume. Arranged entirely alphabetically except for the Biography volume, there are over 2,000 articles covering science, technology, history, geography and the arts. The entries are simply and clearly written providing a basic amount of information, suitable for eight to twelve-year-olds. Illustrations, many of which are photographs, match the text well and have informative captions. A 'See Also' panel at the end of many entries encourages the search for further information and makes cross-referencing easy.

197
WILLIAMS, Brian
Kingfisher First
Encyclopedia
Kingfisher
1991 £12.95 192pp.
0 86272 740 5

Designed for a primary school audience, this first encyclopedia is clearly written and well laid out. Among the entries are several with umbrella headings such as 'The Solar System' which allows for the inclusion of extra topics not listed under separate entries. Explanations are brief which means that there is a limit to the amount of information which can be offered, but they provide a good basic starting point.

1991 PRIZEWINNING CHILDREN'S BOOKS

1991 **Carnegie Medal**
CROSS, Gillian *Wolf* Oxford University Press
1991 **Kate Greenaway Medal**
BLYTHE, Gary *The Whales' Song* Hutchinson
1991 **Children's Book Award**
INKPEN, Mick *Threadbear* Hodder & Stoughton
1991 **Emil/Kurt Maschler Award**
McNAUGHTON, Colin *Have You Seen Who's Just Moved In Next Door?*
Walker Books
1991 **Earthworm Children's Book Award**
CURRY, Jennifer (ed.) *The Last Rabbit* Methuen
1991 **Guardian Children's Fiction Award**
WESTALL, Robert *The Kingdom by the Sea* Methuen
1991 **Macmillan Prize for a Children's Picture Book**
YOUNG, Selina *My Grandpa Has Big Pockets*
1991 **Mother Goose Award**
HARVEY, Amanda *A Close Call* Macmillan
1991 **Signal Poetry Award**
BENSON, Gerard (ed.) *This Poem Doesn't Rhyme* Viking
1991 **Smarties Book Prize**
Overall Winner and 0–5 Years Winner
WADDELL, Martin illus. Helen Oxenbury *Farmer Duck* Walker Books
6–8 Years Winner
NABB, Magdalen *Josie Smith and Eileen* HarperCollins
9–11 Years Winner
RIDLEY, Philip *Krindlekrax* Jonathan Cape
1991 **T.E.S. Information Book Awards**
Senior
MORLEY, Jacqueline, BERGIN, Mark and JAMES, John *An Egyptian Pyramid*
Simon & Schuster Young Books
Junior
PEARCE, Fred and WINTON, Ian *Ian and Fred's Big Green Book*
Kingfisher/Bennett Books
1991 **T.E.S. Schoolbook Award** (2 winners this year)
KITCHEN, David (ed.) *Thin Ice* Oxford University Press
DICKENS, Guy, SCARRETT, Elaine and WILLIAMS, Nick
After the Bomb: Brother in the Land English and Media Centre
1991 **Whitbread Literary Award Children's Novel**
HENDRY, Diana *Harvey Angell* Julia MacRae
1991 **Lancashire County Library Children's Books of the Year Award**
JACQUES, Brian *Mattimeo* Hutchinson

1991 **Kathleen Fidler Award**
HENDRY, George *Greg's Revenge* Blackie
1991 **Science Book Prizes**
Under 14 General Category
BALKWILL, Fran *Cells are Us* and *Cell Wars* HarperCollins
1991 **Tir Na N-Og Awards**
Best Fiction Award
WILLIAMS, Gareth F. *O Ddawns i Ddawns* Y Lolfa
Best Non-Fiction Book of the Year
JENKINS, Geraint H. *Cymru, Ddoe a Heddiw* Oxford University Press

INDEX OF AUTHORS AND ILLUSTRATORS

INDEX OF TITLES

Once [lived happily e

PUT THE MAGIC INTO YOUR BOOK EVENT

"The other week our teacher told us that we would be having a School Book Fair and gave us a colourful leaflet full of books to take home."

"We had great fun preparing for the fair. We were given posters to colour-in, banners to put up, we even ran a competition to design a poster for our favourite books."

"The fair arrived in a long, shiny trailer. The delivery man was ever so friendly and really helpful. He answered all our Headteacher's questions about the fair."

"After the fair arrived each class was allowed to visit it during the week. There were lots of brilliant books there. I bought a great adventure book and mum gave me some extra money to buy a Roald Dahl book."

"We saw the man come and collect the book cases and we waved him off, it was really great."

"When the fair was over we had lots of new books in our library from the money our school earned from the Book Fair."

"I think School Book Fairs are magic, I hope they come back soon."

**Bring the magic of a School Book Fair into your school.
It will give hours of enjoyment to your children.**

SCHOOL BOOK FAIRS
Share the love of reading

School Book Fairs Ltd. 5 Airspeed Road, Priory Industrial Park
Christchurch, Dorset BH23 4HD

Call free:

0800 272321

funny

All children except one

SAIL AWAY WITH
Viking Children's Books

Herbie Whistle by Martin Waddell
0670 83662 1 £4.99

To Be A Ghost by Raymond Wilson
0670 83695 8 £7.99

**Leila's
Magical Monster Party**
by Ann Jungman
0670 83380 0 £4.50

Imagine by Alison Lester
0670 83692 3 £7.99

No Hickory No Dickory No Dock
by John Agard and Grace Nichols
0670 82661 8 £7.99

The Cuckoo Child
by Dick King-Smith
0670 83295 2 £7.99

William and the Wolves
by Kathryn Cave
0670 83487 4 £6.99

**The Puffin Book of
Twentieth-Century Chidren's Verse**
by Brian Patten
0670 81475 X £12.99

The House That Caught A Cold
by Richard Edwards
0670 83583 8 £7.50

GREAT READS *from*

HAMISH HAMILTON CHILDREN'S BOOKS
chosen for the Children's Books of the Year 1992

0241 13100 6 £8.99

0241 13127 8 £8.50

0241 13060 3 £7.99

0241 13032 8 £4.50

0241 12963 X £4.99

0241 13071 9 £3.99

Hamish Hamilton Children's Books
27 Wright's Lane, London, W8 5 TZ

0241 13026 3 £4.50

0241 13137 5 £4.99

BLACKIE CHILDREN'S BOOKS

EVERY WEEK IS CHILDREN'S BOOK WEEK IN A SCHOOL BOOKSHOP

Over 7,500 schools have chosen
BOOKS FOR STUDENTS
School Bookshop Service.

Our stockrange and support service
has developed over the last 25 years in
response to our customers' needs.

If you are thinking about starting
a bookshop in your school, talk to us.
We'll help and advise, without obligation.

Simply telephone 0926 314366
or write to us at

Books for Students Ltd Bird Road Heathcote Warwick CV34 6TB

Look at the Logo.
What do you see?

MANTRA

FOR A WIDER WORLD PERSPECTIVE

MANTRA, publishers of multi-cultural and
dual language books for children, teenagers, adults.

List at least 3 images and you
can win the **PRIZE DRAW**:
3 Mantra books, reviewed in this
Children's Books of the Year.

Send to:
MANTRA PUBLISHING,
5 Alexandra Grove,
London N12 8NU

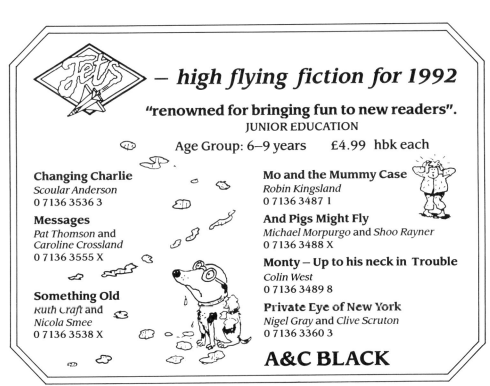

 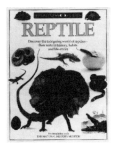 
 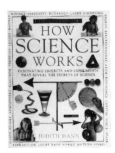

Our *selection of children's books is growing all the time.*

Like your children, our book
selection just gets bigger and bigger.
Our wide range is constantly updated
and expanded with new characters
like Rosie and Jim as well as old favourites
like Postman Pat and Winnie The Pooh.
We also have a huge selection
of books for School and College
and if you can't find the book
you want, we'll order it at no extra
cost especially made to measure.

Wayland

Wayland, one of the leading publishers of children's information books is proud to have had 18 titles selected as

Children's Books of the Year 1992

These books are included in a vast range of entertaining and stimulating series covering many subject areas. Wayland offers vital background reading for all the National Curriculum Key Stages through to GCSE and 'A' level studies. The readers interest is stimulated by well-written texts and colourful photographs and illustrations. Useful glossaries and indexes encourage students to use their information gathering skills.

The 1992 Wayland Catalogue is the comprehensive and colourful guide to all our books, so contact the Sales Department now for your copy.

Wayland (Publishers) Ltd.

61 Western Road, Hove, East Sussex BN3 1JD. Tel: (0273) 722561. Fax: (0273) 29314. Telex: 878170.

GO BANANAS!

Colly's Barn
by Michael Morpurgo
£2.99

Nancy Pocket and the Kidnappers
by Julia Jarman
£2.99

The Big Red Trouble
by Carmen Harris
£2.99

Snow Girl
by Geraldine Kaye
£2.99

Spooky Cottage
by Jean Ure
£2.99

Design a Pram
by Anne Fine
£2.99

AN IMPRINT OF HEINEMANN YOUNG BOOKS

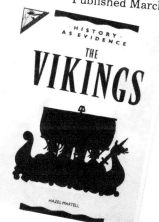